NEIL G. TAMBE

Character By Choice

Letters on Goodness, Courage, and Becoming Better on Purpose

First edition

ISBN: 979-8-9896884-0-1

Editing by Marsha Phillips
Proofreading by Marsha Phillips
Cover art by Keke Shen

This book was professionally typeset on Reedsy.
Find out more at reedsy.com

For Pa, Pops, and Dad.

"Into that heaven of freedom, my Father, let my country awake."

— Rabindranath Tagore,
"Gitanjali 35"

Contents

III   2019

IV   2023

Author's Note

To My Sons...

Let me be honest with you.

I don't know whether I am a good man or if I will be a good father. No one will know until decades after I pass from this earth. What I *do* know is what I want and intend to be. The sentiment I had in Spring 2017, a few months before Robert was born, is the same I have now: to be a good man and a good father.

What does it mean to be good? In this letter and the ones that follow, my goal is to answer that question with thoughtfulness and rigor. I need to walk the walk if I want you three to grow to become good people. The best and perhaps only way I can adequately answer that question—my three sons—is by writing to you directly. You boys are the intended audience of this volume of letters.

When I started writing in 2017, your mother and I only knew of Robert's coming birth, though we dreamed of you both, Myles and Emmett. By God's grace, all three of you are now here as I rewrite this manuscript, in Spring 2022, about three weeks after Emmett's birth. Now, I have edited this volume to address you all collectively.

At the beginning, I wasn't sure if I would share this book with anyone but our family but, as time went on, I began believing its ideas were relevant and worth sharing beyond our home. This book became something I have always wanted from philosophers but felt was missing. As comprehensive as moral philosophy and theology are with the question of "what"—what is good, what is the right choice, etc.—what I found lacking was the question of "how." How do we become the sort of people who do what is good, who make the tough choices to live with goodness in thought and action?

The question of "how" is unglamorous, laborious, and pedantic to answer. It takes a special zealotry to stick with, especially because it requires a tremendous amount of context setting. When you have done all the work, it all seems obvious; yet the question of how we become good people is essential. Perhaps that is why philosophers don't seem to emphasize it, but parents and coaches do. Coming up with the "what" is cool and novel, and once you lay down the "what," it is easy to walk away and leave the details to "lesser minds." However, you have to care deeply enough about a person to get into the muck to help them figure out "how" to do anything. Figuring out the "how" is a much longer, arduous, and entangled process. Here, in these letters, this question of how is what I have been most determined to explore.

Success in securing a goal can be simple if you ask yourself the right questions. Graduate school and good material on management taught me that the first question to ask before starting any journey is: "What result do I want to create?" Once you clarify what success looks like (and doesn't), you can spend your energy working toward that result, instead of wasting time and effort.

As a father, what result do I want to create? I thought about that a lot as Robert's birth approached, and since then as all of you have come into the world. The result I want to create is simple; my duty as a father is two-fold:

1. Love you unconditionally
2. Help you to become good people

That's it. Anything else that comes from my influence in your life is a bonus.

Let me be perfectly up front with you: my mission is not your happiness. Obviously, I hope you will live a healthy, happy, and prosperous life, but goodness and happiness are not the same thing: I am focused on goodness, not happiness. Guaranteeing your health, happiness, and prosperity is a promise I can't keep. It's difficult for me to admit that, but it's true; they are only in your, or God's, hands. I can't even truly promise I will succeed in helping each of you to become good people. I am a mortal, imperfect man, just like you—frustratingly fallible. I may fail at my mission, even if I die trying. But here's what I do promise, right now, in writing; our word is our bond, and these are literally my words: I promise you I will never give up on cultivating the goodness in you or in myself. I will do so as long as I exist in body, mind, and/or spirit. How I approach that task will change as you grow older, but I will never give up. I will make mistakes and learn from them. It is the most important thing I will ever do.

Becoming good is our choice. That is what I have chosen. It is something I am committed to, even if it seems impossible and I may fail regularly. I choose to try to be a better man and to try to help you, my three sons, to become better men. I will never give up on you boys, I swear to you. No matter what happens from here forward, this is my second promise to you: no matter how good or wicked each of you are; no matter how tall or short you are; no matter how wealthy or poor you become; no matter what you look or act like—no matter what—I will always love you, unconditionally, and so will your mother. Always.

Love,
Papa

Introduction

As I reflected on the ideas written in this volume on how to become a good father by becoming a good man myself, my mind was set ablaze. It would be inaccurate to say I thought of them myself. Instead, I found several old ideas that are related but are often left unconnected. My contribution was mostly to connect some dots and tell stories from the heart.

It is my aim to not "bury the lede," which mentors of mine have always chided me about at work. That way, you can quickly decide if you believe this dialogue applies to you. I have discovered that we cannot become good people *directly*. We cannot *will* ourselves to be good, nor can we eat a virtue multivitamin and suddenly think good thoughts, make good choices, and do good deeds. Becoming a good man, unsurprisingly, takes much more work than that. We can work on *specific* virtues. We can do specific things to become more kind, more honest, more curious, more courageous, more humble. We can build the capability to express these virtues just like athletes strengthen their muscles. Much of this book is devoted to identifying how to build the most important virtues in tangible, intentional ways. Said differently, this book is about *becoming better on purpose*.

But which virtues, like muscles, must we build to help us become good people? Consider the difference between exercising our abdomen and chest and exercising our biceps.

Biceps matter but have a narrow purpose. They are vanity muscles, which do not help a person become functionally strong. However, the chest and abdomen are core muscle groups. If an athlete strengthens their chest and abdomen, they build strength for multiple sports. Similarly, we have limited energy and time to maximize the expression of every virtue—or target every muscle in the body. But, just as an athlete focuses mainly on core muscle groups, we can focus on building a few core virtues that help build other virtues. As core virtues become stronger, we can use those core muscles of our character to improve exponentially in our efforts to think good thoughts, make good choices, and do good deeds. In other words, if we focus on a few core virtues, we can have a greater possibility of becoming a better person across different domains and circumstances, in our real, daily lives. In my eyes, those core virtues are curiosity, courage, and persistence. I will spend a significant amount of time explaining why they matter; but first, I will offer you my best rationale for why we should care about being good people.

Being a good person matters to me, but I cannot assume it will matter to you. You, presumably, need more of a reason than "that's what our faith calls us to do" or "because I said so." Otherwise, I'm 100% positive you won't do it. We all need a good "why" to do the hard but important work of building core virtues and using that strength of character to become good people. Articulating that "why" is the focus of the early parts of this book.

We should be good people because, to function, communities depend on a combination of trust and rules, and there is a tradeoff between the two. If we want to have fewer rules in our community, and therefore have more freedom, we need to have more trust. And to have a trusting community, people in the community have to be good people. Beyond faith and an intrinsic sense of righteousness, even beyond being a good father, becoming a good person matters to me because I care about freedom. I want to live in a society that needs less rules and feels like a trustworthy place.

I first read *East of Eden* by John Steinbeck in high school; it is the most important novel I have ever read. It contains a most important idea: *timshel*: "thou mayest." Lee, one of the book's characters, tells of a biblical passage discussing man's conquering of sin: the sixteen verse in the fourth chapter of Genesis. Lee finds that different translations of the Bible present a different understanding of what God says about man's ability to conquer sin. One translation, the King James Version, indicates, *thou shall conquer sin*, implying that a man overcoming his sinful ways is an inevitability. It's a done deal. The American Standard Version indicates that *thou must conquer sin*, implying that God commands man to overcome his sin. In this version, it is not an inevitability—it's an imperative.

These two translations, being radically different, leave Lee flummoxed. To remedy this, he, with the help of a few wise old men, goes back to the original Hebrew scripture in hopes of deciphering an accurate understanding of the verse's intent. There, Lee finds the word *timshel* where the verse, Steinbeck reveals, translates to *"thou mayest"* conquer sin. Therefore, conquering our sins is not an inevitability and it's not an imperative—it's a choice! Steinbeck conveys that the Biblical God says we may conquer our sins; it is in our hands. Our character, and all that we become, is up to us.

* * *

ix

I

2017

1

The Tension Between Goodness and Power

**If you don't choose,
our culture will choose for you.**

April 6, 2017

My Sons,

In Spring 2012, my life was a mess. It didn't appear that way to most (even me), but a few people realized I was struggling—and they cared. *That* changed the trajectory of my life, that little act of noticing mattered; it was a nudge that put me back on the long path before I could drift indefinitely toward becoming a man I did not want to become. That spring, I was making choices I didn't even know were bad, and that gracious love likely prevented me from squandering years of my life. It might have been a long time before I realized I had lost myself. But I'm getting ahead of myself here.

Trying to become a good person is like taking a long walk in the woods—it's winding, strenuous, not always well marked;

there are many diversions, and no clear destination. It is not a place where we arrive and then simply declare we are good. It's a walk where we just keep going, one foot in front of the other, and it can be chilly, rainy, uncomfortable—not every day is sunny.

I learned the word *righteousness* at age ten or younger. It was a word I had heard lots of Indian aunties and uncles say during *Svādhyāya*, Sanskrit for "self-study" (and what my Sunday school for Indian children was called). When those aunties and uncles taught us prayers, commandments, and the like, the word *righteousness* was often translated. My father, your *Dada*, also used it. I can hear him, still, with his particular pronunciation of the word, talking to me about the *rite-chus* path. This idea of taking a long walk in the woods, you see, boys, is an old idea in our culture. To me, talking about being a good person, going on a long walk in the woods, taking the righteous path—whatever you want to call it—is not just words and metaphors, but *dharma*, spiritual duty. It is a long walk down an often difficult but righteous path, but it is still a choice, for you, like it was to me, my father before me, and his father before him. In our family, all your aunts and uncles and grandparents had this choice. This is a choice we have had to make: to walk the righteous path or not. To do the right thing, or not. Will we take the long walk, day after day, and try to be good people, or will we not? This is the great choice of our lives. We have to choose.

In Spring 2012, the season just before I started dating your mother, I was living in Detroit with your Aunt Jenny. We lived in a building called the New Amsterdam Lofts (once an old penny slot machine factory) at the corner of 2nd Avenue and Amsterdam, at the south end of the New

Center neighborhood. The neighborhood was situated in a sort of no man's land because it wasn't in the urban core of downtown surrounded by skyscrapers and boutiques. It wasn't a residential neighborhood dotted with single family homes; rather, it was a mix of tired residential buildings, new lofts for uppity people like me, lovable dive bars, government buildings, a wonderful old theater, and too many parking lots. It was a bit of everything. In those times, Detroit was simmering with new people and ideas. Of course, it still is, probably more so, but there was a different sense of possibility then because it was the beginning of the most recent cycle of great change: bankruptcy; major real estate projects; and overdue investments in streetscapes and green spaces.

I was also in transition. I was exploring, learning, and more than anything, trying to find your mother. At 24 years old, the peak of my youthful invincibility, I was old enough to vote and hold down a salaried job, but young enough to hit the bars and never have a hangover last more than a day. It was a special time in my life, formative, even if too self-indulgent— the first time I was part of something objectively big. The scale of the city, quite literally, was larger than anything I had ever encountered beyond visiting Delhi and New York on family vacations. For a suburban, straight-laced kid like me, who never felt at home anywhere, living in the city felt like a slightly rebellious adventure. Detroit was, and still is, something altogether different than Rochester (where I grew up) and Ann Arbor (where I went to school). But beyond the urbanity, size, grit, and gravity of its history, I felt a mysterious warmth in Detroit. Over time, I learned that this warmth came from everyday Detroiters —that soft but consistent glow, radiating from everyone I encountered, was nothing short of magical. For the first time in my life, despite being an Indian American yuppie in an aging Black, White, and Latino city, people treated me like I belonged there. Detroit felt more like home to me than any other place I had ever lived.

Your Aunt Jenny and I heard about the building in New Center because your Uncle Jeff and Aunt Laura lived there, so we moved there. It was like living in the dorms with a friend a few doors down. Beyond the collegiate energy of living under the same roof as close friends, moving to the New Amsterdam Lofts was a very important decision for reasons I wasn't aware of at the time. I was lonely. I worked too much and spent too much money at the bar. I was studying to take the GMAT for admission to business school, which I naively thought was the magical elixir that would fix all my personal and professional woes. I thought I needed something new and bigger in my life. Luckily, your Uncle Jeff and Aunt Laura, who lived down the hall, knew better. I didn't need anything new and fancy—I needed to get back to basics. That spring, your Uncle Jeff and Aunt Laura had me, your Aunt Jenny, and Uncle Mike over for dinner and bible study. At the time, I wasn't practicing any religion, but I always enjoyed learning from the wisdom of any philosophy or theology, and I still do. Besides that, I got to spend time and have lovely meals with all of them.

And that's what my life consisted of: working too much; drinking; studying (unsuccessfully) for the GMAT; chasing girls at bars in Detroit; and hanging out with your Uncle Jeff, Aunt Laura, Aunt Jenny, and Uncle Mike. That May, I finally took the GMAT, which I had been studying for months. When I pushed the submit button at the end of the test, I knew I had choked.

That night, I had planned a bar night with friends. I was

so stressed, I drank beyond my usual limits. A girl I had just stopped dating was there; the night transpired, and I woke up in her apartment. Mind you, this was not something I did. I managed to get through college without a hookup. And, even if I tried, I was unsuccessful at getting girls I didn't know to even talk to me, let alone anything else. And, despite being caught up in the twenty-something bar and dating culture, deep down I didn't want to "hook up," I just thought that was a way to not feel lonely. What I wanted was to find your mother, who I knew was out there, and who, by that time, I had already met and started to fall in love with. I wanted a long-term relationship. I wanted a girlfriend who would be my wife someday. I didn't want a casual relationship, physically or emotionally. The night I had was not reflective of the man I wanted to be. More importantly, it was wrong and hurtful. Rekindling a relationship I knew I wasn't interested in long-term was wrong. It was unfair to the woman I had dated because it revived something we had tried, talked about, and had transitioned amicably. In retrospect, having intimacy with someone consensually is not something to be ashamed of, though randomly hooking up consensually is destructive in other ways. That I had agreed to being friends and had broken that promise burdened me with guilt and shame.

The next morning, in the middle of May, was my low point. I was scared about graduate school applications because my GMAT score was at the low end of an acceptable range. I was in a job that was devouring me. I was lonely and the one leg I had left to stand on—that at least I was not a jackass—was now wobbly. My footing as a person and a man was slipping and I was falling. A few weeks later, at one of those dinners at Uncle Jeff and Aunt Laura's down the hall, we skipped bible study. They must have sensed it was time, finally, and just talked. That Sunday night, around their sturdy wooden table, *I talked.* Everyone waited quietly while I broke in two, right in front of them. For the first time in my adult life, I was honest with myself and with them. That moment, around the wooden table, in the ground floor loft apartment, in the middle of New Center in Detroit was where *this* story, the one in this volume, began. It was the true start of my adult life, the inflection point from which all others were borne.

Strangely, despite its significance, I remember little of that night. All I remember is weeping uncontrollably as I accepted, for the first time, how lonely and depressed I was. But as I drew my gaze up from the plate and wood grain in front of me, my eyes were opened. I saw that there were people in this world who loved me and would not let me slip away.

I am telling you this, not to make me seem more relatable to you in my bachelor days, or to try to be a "cool dad," or to have a self-indulgent catharsis, or to make you feel sorry for me; it's to contrast what happened before that day with everything that happened after. A story must start at its beginning. After that day, your Uncle Jeff gave me the book, *Emotionally Healthy Spirituality*, one of the most important gifts I have ever received, which helped me to start living with my mental state and emotions instead of suppressing them. It restarted my exploration of a belief in God and a spiritual life. After that day, after a long break, I finally started on the long walk again. I stopped chasing girls and refocused on having deep, healthy relationships, including a deep friendship with your mother. Your mother and I started dating and eventually married. I graduated from my master's program and had the courage to walk away from a lucrative job with a lot of prestige that would have strained our marriage. I started to improve my relationship with my family, especially your Dada and Dadi. Your mother and I adopted your big dog-brother, Riley, and moved into the first home you would ever know. I gained and became enmeshed with a new family more globally distributed than the family I inherited from my parents. I started running, reading, and writing again. Perhaps, most importantly, I started my journey as a recovering yuppie, and tried to obsess less and less over work, career, money, and status.

One of the greatest things that happened was you three, our sons. As I write this, we are on a plane from France with your Mimi and Granddad, your Aunt Lyssi, and our France-based family. Your mom is pregnant with Robert and sleeping in the seat next to me. We are on our way to your Aunt Ellie's wedding in England. Your Uncle Toph has just moved to Japan to teach English. Your Dadi is at home in Rochester, sleeping, and your Dada is watching over you from the heavens.

You, my sons, are already loved. There are so many good things that have happened, and so many are left to come.

—

I can't achieve my mission of being a good father to you three without being a good man myself. The process of becoming a good man is so important it cannot be left to chance. I'm writing not for you but for me, so I can make sure I understand what a good man is and how to become one, *on purpose, intentionally*, so I'm prepared when you all arrive. I'm taking loose thoughts and making them clear and specific enough to put into action. If you or others find value in it, that's even better. I hope you (and anyone else) can learn from my experiences so you can make more useful mistakes than I

9

have.

A second lesson has taken me years to figure out: understanding why my life was in such disarray that spring, and how it got back on track. I realized I was lusting for power. In my experience, if we eliminate artificial, impractical, purely academic distinctions, the behavior of mortal men is driven by two influences that often come into tension with each other: power and goodness. This tradeoff between the desire for power and the desire to be good has been the driving force of my moral life. Navigating this tradeoff is not a small act. Many of our choices bear little consequence in how we define ourselves or how others see who we are, but whether to take the long walk down the righteous path defines how I see myself and how others perceive me. I could eat a few grapes while grocery shopping without paying for them, but I don't, that's an easy choice. I could eat half a dish at a restaurant, claim there is a hair in it, and weasel out of paying full price, but I don't, that's an easy choice. A lot of times, choosing goodness over power, money, status, convenience, etc. is not hard. When it's easy to be good, I, you, and everybody else just does it. But sometimes, choosing goodness over power is *really hard.* Often, we must choose between what we know is right and a wrong that gives us more resources, status, or influence. It's hard to choose goodness over power in the schoolyard when you must choose whether to join a bully or stand up to him. It's hard in business when profits come at the cost of a harmful (but legal) externality. It's hard in politics when competing interests jockey for support on an upcoming vote. It's hard to choose goodness over power when family members are figuring out how to divide an inheritance fairly or how to take care of elderly parents. Sometimes, power and goodness are not in conflict, and that's great. But for many consequential decisions, power and goodness are in tension with each other. In these letters, we will focus on navigating goodness and power when it's hard; you don't need my help if it's easy.

I define power (for the purposes of our conversation) based on its function. For a mortal man, the practical function of power is to coerce, compel, or influence what he cannot control. In this world, the league of things we cannot control is vast: we cannot control the weather or the quaking of the earth. We cannot control how we are treated by others and whether others intend to hurt us or not. We cannot control the payout of the genetic lottery endowed to us by our parents. We cannot control famine, disease, or the absolute safety of our water supply. We cannot control threats of violence, or the amount of respect we receive, or the degree to which we will be bullied and exploited by individuals or groups with more power than us. This list goes on. Why would we not want to have control over these things? Isn't it rational and natural to avoid death and suffering? Isn't it reasonable to fear for our delicate, precarious mortality? Does anyone like being exploited, bullied, or disrespected by other people? Because we resist suffering and death, power is our coping strategy to temper the difficult things we cannot control, making power alluring and desirable; therefore, to seek power is rational.

Goodness, however, is harder to define, but I have come to define it based on how it feels: there is a certain peace and deep pleasure that comes from being good. It feels good to be pure of heart and soul, to be a creature that doesn't cause pain or suffering to other people, other creatures, or the earth. Despite knowing I am capable of being a monster that hurts

11

others, this is not what I want to become. I want to bring beauty and joy. I do not know where that desire comes from, but I know it is there, and I have heard and seen echoes of the same feeling in others. The ability to manifest this through action is what I mean by goodness. Goodness is taking the talk of that feeling and making it walk.

Even if I could substantiate why I feel this deeply rooted inclination for goodness, does anyone need a justification to be truthful or to love purely? Do we need an excuse to do what's right? Do we require a reason to contribute to the beauty in the world?

I grapple with the tension between power and goodness. They are not pure opposites like hot and cold; there is no trade-off required based on how the words are defined, but there *is* one—in practice. Sometimes the choice that gives us more power makes us less good. Why? To illuminate, I find the expression, "power corrupts," informative. Power comes in many forms and can corrupt, but the corruption boils down to the same mechanism. If you have power, you may grow accustomed or favorable toward it, and come to need it and become afraid of losing it. It can become an addiction. For example, I like how it feels to be a manager rather than the entry-level employee on my team. I like having money in my pocket over being broke. I like having the electricity to run an air conditioning unit over being beholden to the breeze coming through our bedroom window. I'm afraid of losing these advantages. In humans, power can cause a sort of addiction to the spoils it provides.

Humans don't like losing things they need or are addicted to. Just like having an addiction to a substance, they will go to extraordinary lengths to keep it, even if it means lying, cheating, or stealing. The tension between power and goodness lies in the moments of potential loss. We cannot always preserve power in a way that's consistent with good thoughts, choices, and deeds.

Power that can corrupt comes in many forms. In the form of authority, where the holder can legally use force or administer sanctions for non-compliance. In the form of money, where its holder can exchange it for goods, services, or loyalty. From status, where the person in a high position can persuade others to act according to his or her choosing. In the form of physical fitness or longevity, where the fit body can outmuscle or outlast another.

In Spring 2012, I wanted to be a good son, brother, and nephew, but I wasn't speaking to my family, even your Dada and Dadi, with any regularity. I was trying to find my soulmate—your mother—but I was hitting the bars twice a weekend and indiscriminately trying to win over any nice, cute girl I came across. I wanted to do work I was proud of and make other people's lives better, but I was arrogantly and ambitiously trying to get promoted and climb the career ladder as quickly as possible. I was a mortal lusting for power; also, trying to be a good person. I was at war with myself. Trying to have both power and goodness was tearing my soul in two.

—

When power and goodness come into tension, I am asking you to choose a path. You may think you can have both, and that's true to an extent, like working a job to earn money or status in a way that doesn't come at the cost of goodness. To survive, some amount of power, in whatever form it comes, is essential so you can have food, shelter, and clothing. Our individual lives and our entire civilization depend on power. Choosing "neither" isn't possible. If you don't choose, our culture will choose for you. Why? Because our culture talks more about power than about goodness.

In my life, I spent too much time chasing power. Most of the time, I didn't know I was doing it because I wasn't making a conscious choice: I was letting society choose for me. I made many mistakes and wasted so much time choosing power. I regret it. Luckily, I was touched by the grace of God. Right around the time I met your mother, your uncles and aunts helped me to change what I was choosing at just the right time. With their help, I was ready to become friends with, date, and then marry your mother. They helped me to get back on the path of goodness before I did anything that would push your mother away. I was gifted with a second chance, a second life. I will not squander it.

So, my sons, I propose that you *choose goodness.* However, it's not as simple as choosing. Goodness doesn't grow on trees, and there's no magic virtue-inducing pharmaceutical to take. It's not something we can say out loud and it just happens. There are no shortcuts or free lunches when it comes to choosing goodness. We must build up the muscle of our core virtues so we have the strength of character to choose goodness when we need it the most. Commit to the path, even though it is intimidating. Do the arduous emotional labor required to build the core muscle groups of virtue (curiosity, courage, and persistence), to trust the process, and to put in the hours to strengthen your character up front. *Choose the work.* If you choose the work, goodness will come. Before we get into *how,* I will explain *why* you should choose to strengthen your character, and choose it over power. That's where we will begin in my next letter to you.

Love,
Your Papa

* * *

2

Why Goodness?

**Living in a society
with freedom depends on goodness.**

April 7, 2017

My Sons,

If I am a good father, I will have taught you to think for yourself and to pursue the skeptical inquiry of new ideas (even ones propagated by me). I assume you are bright enough to be skeptical. So, let's start with the question: *Why goodness?* The first answer is that of God and religion: we should walk toward goodness because God says so. The two traditions I am most familiar with, Hinduism and Christianity, are clear about goodness and the right way to live. Christianity talks about living and learning from Jesus' example of love and sacrifice, while Hinduism talks about one's dharma—our spiritual duties. The bit of exposure I have had to Buddhism suggests that power shouldn't be the anchor of one's life or decision making because power comes and goes, and one shouldn't attach oneself to things that are not permanent.

Even in my limited knowledge of these faiths, I cannot imagine a single religious tradition that would advocate for power over goodness in the way we have laid out the concepts. Jesus did not talk about "making that money." Hindu scripture does not outline the aims of our lives in a way that indicates that playing the field or getting turnt up with bottle service at the club is what we should be doing. None of the faiths I have known, though different in some ways, advocate the notion of a power-centric life. Rather, they advocate goodness or similar concepts. Despite their mystery, I find the thinking and philosophy underpinning different religious traditions to be wise and helpful. Interpreted in their purest forms, these traditions teach how to live. They have lasted and been refined over thousands of years. All traditions that have withstood the test of time bend toward goodness, and if the world's religions have reached a general consensus that goodness is the path to take, that endorsement is strong justification with little need for additional evidence. Still, I cannot assume religious thought is something you will find persuasive. Many people, especially my age, have zero trust in religious traditions and reject them. You might be skeptical, too.

To justify walking toward goodness instead of power, we can also make what I call the "tortoise and the hare" argument: "When you do the right thing, things work out better in the end," which suggests that goodness leads to better outcomes in the long term, just as the tortoise won the race because of his consistent effort and the hare's arrogant attitude. In the case of teams and organizations, it's the simple idea of "doing the right thing is better for business anyway." This argument was often made to me by classmates and professors in graduate school. In business schools and in the business press, those that make the tortoise and the hare argument for goodness suggest that being honest, good to employees, and good to society leads to better business results. Doing the right thing, they say, is good for the bottom line. When you do right by your employees, they work harder and are more loyal. When you do right by customers and society, it forces your team to produce more innovative products and services, putting the business on a path to sustainable profits. When you do the right thing, the business is less likely to have a scandal or break the law—events that can be devastating to an enterprise. Good, ethical companies, they said, have greater goodwill with employees, customers, and society, which pays off in the long run. I agree.

One of the things your Dada said to me all through my life is: "Neil, you are a very capable person." In my heart, even though I haven't met you boys yet, I know you are very capable people. I am confident in the decisions you will make about goodness, power, and any other matter. But we all are human and need support to choose the work and walk toward goodness throughout our lifetimes. It is easy to become more about self-interest than nobility. If our justification for walking toward goodness is that it benefits us, how do we know we will stay committed to goodness rather than benefits? Could we really trust ourselves to walk toward goodness when it is costly or has a long run time before "pay off?" What if walking toward goodness was detrimental to our interests, would we still walk that path? Here is the most persuasive argument I can think of for goodness: we should walk toward goodness because living in a society with freedom depends on it.

—

Imagine you are living alone in the wilderness. You can even call it the state of nature in a nod to Hobbes' *Leviathan*. When you decided to live there, you chose to renounce society and never interact with another human again. You're on your own, in the fullest sense of the expression. To survive, you need food, water, and shelter from weather and predators. Every tool, lean-to, or piece of clothing you need, you produce yourself; every food you eat, you must hunt, gather or grow, and cook yourself.

But in nature, you are also free. You have no attachments to other people, no commitments to hem and haw about; you do not have to worry about theft or murder. There is nobody to disrupt your solitude because *there is nobody*. Which also means there is nobody to tend to your wounds, nobody to talk to, nobody to work with to secure food, water, and shelter, nobody to borrow from or trade with. There is nobody to love.

Say you decide you don't want your existence to be strictly self-determined. You choose to create a community so someone has your back, so you would not feel terribly lonely all the time. Let's say you form a small tribe of less than 10 people. If you were to join a tribe, even a small one, I am sure you would quickly discover that no human is perfect and that relationships are not without friction. Even though everyone in the tribe has good intentions, surely there will inevitably be a conflict between members of your tribe. The first couple of conflicts are small, so they are mostly ignored or easily resolved. This development, that your tribe can resolve conflict, is critical. This resolution of conflict is building trust and allowing cooperation to happen. Through this cooperation, the tribe is solving problems and learning.

19

Your tribe continues to work together and is prospering. It's growing organically, more children are surviving, and other people you come across want to join you and the other founders. Life is good in your tribe.

More good news! The tribe has grown to about 30 people. There are more people with diverse skills, which is good because the tribe has a greater ability to survive the treachery of nature. The tribe's rate of learning is increasing because of the newfound diversity. There is more surplus time and resources, which leaves room for the greater development of technologies, art, and culture. But this growth also has challenges. The more diverse the tribe, the more opinions there are. Conflict happens more often now, but it's mostly handled and tolerated. Luckily, the people in the tribe still know each other and there are enough peacemakers with social credibility to help resolve conflicts. Life is still good.

But alas, the fact that we are mere mortals and imperfect has finally caught up with us. A few members of the tribe have a dispute about the equal distribution of food that is not resolved. In fact, it leads to an explosive argument and ends with fisticuffs. This has never happened before, and our tribe is looking to its most respected members to figure out a solution. Everyone knows this is only the first argument, not the last. So, the tribe decides to do something never needed before: it makes a *rule* for how food is distributed so everyone gets their fair share, and nobody goes hungry. With the new rule in place, all is good again. This idea of having a "rule" is a huge innovation and has gone over well across the entire tribe. After a close call, life is once again good.

However, as time passes, the imperfect humanity of the tribe's members continues. Trouble is starting to brew. The tribe has grown again, and there are now people who break the food-sharing rule on a regular basis. It's just not understood by younger and newer members of the tribe who weren't around or alive for its founding. The tribe's most respected members meet again and come up with a more innovative solution. They develop a new type of rule called a *punishment* that imposes negative consequences on those who break the rule and don't share food equitably. This innovation—punishment—is very effective. The tribe is thriving again. Peace persists and the rate of learning, growth, diversity, and prosperity continues to increase. The tribe has more members and more surplus than you could even imagine! Thank goodness you decided to leave the state of nature!

There has been a long peace in the village (it's too big to be called a "tribe" now), but it has just been broken. There is an offender of the village's new rule against stealing food and water. The village's elders informally discuss the incident and decide on an appropriate way to have restoration and restitution with the village: two extra days of labor during the harvest. This is reasonable, given the severity of the violation and historical precedent—but this offender says no to the punishment and starts fighting some of the village elders. The relative physical strength of someone in the village now matters because, even after adding rules and punishments to prevent and manage conflict, some issues still end in violence. As it turns out, for a system of rules and punishment to work, a mix of legitimacy, voluntary compliance, and enforcement is required. This new development, challenging the norms of the village and its elders with violence, is bad. Thus far, informal social systems to manage conflict in the village has largely worked. The rules and punishments have been fair,

21

but now the benevolent approach to handling disputes—with members of the tribe utilizing a few rules and punishments but mostly resolving disputes on their own—no longer works.

There had been a long period of growth where relationships between people, social norms, and agreements based on honor had been enough. During that period, a limited set of rules to supplement informal systems of conflict resolution had also been enough. But as the community has grown, more and more disputes are now being resolved through violence, and social norms, relationships and a limited set of rules are no longer enough to regulate behavior in the village. As a result, villagers are afraid to go about their lives. Everyone is tired of it and wants the violence to stop. So the village elders think about it and come up with another idea to address this new challenge of rule enforcement and legitimacy. This time, in addition to the council of village elders serving as a decision body, the village has designated a few members into two types of special roles. One role is that of "rule-enforcers," who are permitted to use force to uphold the rules and carry out punishments. The other is that of "rule-revisers," who get the opinions of everyone in the tribe and revise the rules on everyone's behalf. This is another big innovation and change in the village, which now has a rudimentary administrative state. This new system of "government" works and is considered legitimate. Life in the tribe is good again. Violent people calm down and the written rules are limiting but are not *too* onerous.

More time passes.

The system of rule-enforcers and rule-revisers has been working well, but the tribe is realizing how hard it is to revise rules and enforce them fairly. Rule-revisers aren't writing perfect rules, so rule-enforcers must be flexible. Sometimes they must use discretion when enforcing the rules, and sometimes the rules are pushed to the edge of being enforced fairly. The rule enforcers do not let people break the rules, but sometimes it's hard to not bend them for unforeseen circumstances. The system of government is still working, but it's being tested.

More time passes; the village keeps evolving. Luckily, the village has cycled through several cohorts of competent, honest, and benevolent leadership. The village is getting comfortable with this regime of rule-revisers and rule-enforcers, and because daily life has become less violent, it's growing again. There's another influx of villagers with diverse experiences and skills from other places. This aids growth but adds tension to the system because some of these new villagers don't understand why the village's social norms and system of rules and punishments are so important, how it works, or how they should behave as citizens. Some of them are exceptionally good at farming. They dramatically increase crop yields, having developed a new technology of watering fields called irrigation. They are starting to teach others this new agricultural practice. Despite their not understanding the village's social norms or rules, the rest of the village is happy to have them around and to learn from them.

But their technological development has caused a problem. There are now some villagers—the developers of the irrigation techniques and those they have taught—whose plots of land yield several times more crops than everyone else's in the village. One villager wants to keep a portion of his bumper crop, even though the tribe's earliest rule compels equitable food distribution. Word of a brewing conflict is starting to get out, so the village elders dispatch a rule-enforcer to enforce the rule and resolve the issue.

Upon arrival, the prolific farmer offers a proposal. He asks the rule-enforcer to bend the rules to let him keep some of his bumper crop. He's earned it with his superior skills, and he is teaching the irrigation technique to others, so it's only fair to keep some of the surplus, right? The prolific farmer even offers to "share" some of this haul with the rule-enforcer if he agrees to this "alternative resolution."

The rule-enforcer struggles with this decision but is enticed by having extra food. He has a family to support and there are still sometimes shortages in the village. Will he let this prolific farmer keep a portion of his surplus and share a few of the spoils, or will he enforce the village rules? He must choose.

—

As we have come to a very consequential point in this thought experiment, let me recap the key points. We started in nature and moved to a small tribe. Our community grew and adapted to small conflicts, then grew and adapted again, this time by making rules, however imperfect. As the tribe grew into a village, it adapted again by creating a rudimentary form of "government"—rule-revisers and rule-enforcers—to prevent conflict from devolving into violence. This propelled the village to grow even more and a new influx of people, technology, and diverse skillsets created surplus resources that were unevenly distributed.

Now we are at the point where a regular person, who happens to be a public servant, has a choice: to enforce the rules fairly or to be tempted by a corrupt proposition. Ideally, we would have never gotten to this point because the village would not have needed a government to resolve disputes and promulgate rules. But our tribe is made up of mere mortals, so rules and enforcement are needed. What should we do?

This thought experiment accentuates a deeply embedded challenge in human societies, that I call the *corruption problem*: we must decide between enriching ourselves at the cost of others, or adhering to laws and principles that preserve trust, fairness, and positive social norms. It's the decision we face when choosing if to shoplift a candy bar from a store. Or deciding if to let a colleague take the blame for a failed project. Or if to cheat in a relationship, even though "nobody will ever know." Large or small, corruption has the same key feature: we have some power and must decide whether to abuse it or sacrifice and walk toward goodness instead.

But there's a larger game at play here. The corruption problem doesn't just exist in the day-to-day life of regular people like us. It exists and is affected at the societal level—which brings us back to our village.

There are four general strategies for affecting the corruption problem at the *societal level*. The first approach is to create abundance. If our village, for example, has more food than it needs, the rule-enforcer has little upside to agreeing to a corrupt deal because he doesn't feel the pressure of scarcity and doubt regarding feeding his family. Also, if there is abundance, the prolific farmer also has less reason to keep more for himself. (We will talk more about abundance later. It's not a solution to the corruption problem, per se, but it does lessen the tension that creates opportunity and the hunger for abuse of power. If a society, as a whole, has abundance, the tension that pushes people toward corruption lessens.)

The second approach to affect the corruption problem is homogenization. It is so dangerous and slippery a path,

I only mention it as an example of what to avoid at all costs. As you may have noticed in our village thought experiment, as the village grew, diversity increased. That diversity accelerated growth, but it also increased conflict. To affect the corruption problem, we could lessen the diversity in the village, which could lessen the conflict and tension on the village's political system by increasing cohesion. But, if we were to do that, we might not have breakthroughs like the one of irrigation, which is a huge net benefit to the village. By increasing homogenization, we would likely sacrifice growth and abundance.

But there is a darker dynamic beyond less growth and abundance. Even if we were to increase homogenization, what would have to be true for it to happen? It may start benignly with attempts to create shared values and helping villagers assimilate into that common identity. But that wouldn't be enough because, in a sufficiently large group, there will be outliers—whether its new émigrés to the village or descendants of one of the village's founding families. Mortals are not identical. So, what then? To achieve homogenization beyond assimilation, the village would have to go to greater lengths. Would we create nostalgic narratives about the good old days? Would we find ways to arrest people who are part of those diverse groups and keep them contained? Would we prevent "outsiders" from marrying the "pure bloods"? Would we ban books with "controversial" ideas? Would we segregate "other" groups to prevent the prevailing culture from being "polluted"? If all that doesn't sufficiently homogenize the village, would we find ways to dehumanize those who are different so there is justified enslavement or genocide?

Cohesion does have its value and merits for lessening

tension on the village's political system, but when it's hijacked, which can easily happen, it becomes a road to hell paved with good intentions. So, to affect the corruption problem, the first two approaches certainly have their challenges. Abundance is a terrific idea, but it is difficult to achieve in practice. Cohesion and homogenization are risky and dangerous. So, what's left?

A third approach is to create institutions. The village could create rules and oversight bodies to ensure those with disproportionate power are watched. In the village, maybe that means having transparent records and documentation. Or maybe a rotation of powers so the same rule-enforcers do not interact with the same farmers when managing food distribution. Maybe there's a regulatory body selected to seg-regate the duties of collecting farmers' crops and distributing them. There are lots of variations of what an institutional intervention could look like, but the underlying principles are the same: design the system so there are less opportunities to abuse power, then watch the people who have a lot of it. The path of institutions affects the corruption problem, not by lessening tension, but by regulating moments that corruption might occur.

The last general strategy is the path of character. Our village could try to cultivate people—whether it's everyday citizens or members of the government—who are good and who do the right thing, even under duress or temptation. In our example, this would mean the prolific farmer would never offer the rule-enforcer the proposal of sharing the spoils of the bumper crop, and the rule-enforcer would not entertain such an offer because both know it is wrong. After all, if the people in the village treat each other with goodness and behave with good character, the culture would be such that everyone is less susceptible to corruption, is more trusting, and fewer rules and institutions would be needed in the first place. Like other paths we have examined, the path of character affects corruption by lessening tension. This leaves us to decide how we will deal with the corruption problem.

In our country, today, we use two general strategies: building institutions and building character, at least to some degree. By my observation, the path of institutions, with all its controls, oversight, competition, and unbundling of power, has been prominent during my lifetime. People my age (at least folks I hang around) talk much about "changing the system," which is another way of saying, "let's build bigger and better institutions." *If we could just change how rules are made and enforced*, they say, *the world would be a better place. Our laws and policies and the power asymmetries they create are the problem.*

But changing the system is not a trivial matter. Over time, the system has become larger and more entrenched because our country has become larger and more complex. Moreover, many people here have low levels of trust in government and other power-wielding institutions; therefore, fewer people participate in the reform process, making it easier for corrupting influences to go unchecked.

Finally, when we change the system or make new rules, it doesn't always go as planned. Sometimes the changes we make turn out worse due to imperfect policies—we are mere mortals after all. Changing the system is something we surely have to do, but it's really hard and it doesn't always work.

The strategy of building character deals with corruption at its root, shaping our society to be driven more by goodness than by power. But it takes time, dialogue, and compassion to shape the people's motivations. Changing people's minds without using power or coercion takes vision, repetition, and patience. It's not possible to force anyone into walking the path of goodness because, for a culture of goodness to last, it must be a choice everyone freely makes after looking deeply into their own soul.

Let me return to the original purpose of this thought experiment about the state of nature, tribes, and corruption: why the world needs us to choose the path of goodness. Humans have two difficult problems when we live in a community of others rather than in the state of nature. We must ensure the community doesn't devolve into a state of violence (i.e., by creating rules, and institutions to enforce those rules), and that the corrupting influence of power doesn't cause the system of government to rot from within.

Up until your mom and I found out we were having you, I had been reading, writing, and thinking about institutions, how to create and run them well, and about changing the system to make sure they do. However, since I have been reflecting on fatherhood and writing these letters to you, I have grown more confused about institutions and their role in society. I have come to see them more for what they are: an intentional concentration of power bounded by rules, controls, and systems to ensure it is wielded without abuse.

As I have challenged myself to think about institutions through the lens of power and goodness, I have cooled my singular focus on building better ones. I don't like the world I foresee an institution-heavy approach would create because they manage, regulate, and constrain freedoms. I don't want our world to be one where, to resolve conflict, prevent violence and deter corruption, we stack rule on top of rule, penalty on top of penalty, oversight board after oversight board, and check after balance. I'm not sure that would ultimately lead to less conflict, violence, and corruption. This is what makes building character and moving toward a vision where our community and culture chooses to walk the path of goodness so important to me. Such a culture prevents conflict, violence, and corruption in the first place and reduces the need for institutions. To be sure, building character and a goodness-motivated culture is at least as difficult as reforming institutions. We will always need better institutions—our society's size requires it—but if it were possible to make our world a place that builds character and a culture of goodness, I would much rather live in that world.

The schism you must be feeling, as to how your individual choice to choose goodness ladders up to the community's aggregate choice, is not lost on me. It's hard to see how individual acts affect the broader culture, but they *are* connected—individual actions affect perceptions of what is normal and vice versa. The actions you take do not necessarily compel others to behave a certain way, but they have influence because our actions shape what is normal. For example, if you lie, others you consistently interact with will think it is more normal to lie than they otherwise would have had you not lied. If you lie consistently, it will give others more implicit, social permission to lie more than they otherwise would. Over time, seemingly little acts generate a feedback loop that will eventually be powerful enough to shift what constitutes normal behavior. Conversely, if you tell the truth, and do it consistently, it will give others the implicit, social permission to tell the truth.

Your actions have reverberations beyond your own life. The book, *How Behavior Spreads: The Science of Complex Contagions*, by Damon Centola, explains this complex system dynamic of how behaviors spread from neighborhood to neighborhood. This observation of how our actions affect others and how culture affects us is especially important to keep in mind because of the time we live in. Social technologies make it easier and faster to influence what's normal. I've noticed that the terrible parts of our humanity are the ideas that spread wider and faster, and so our perception of what is normal gets skewed. If *we* (you and me specifically, as well as "society") do not choose goodness, being good will become less normal, perhaps even abnormal, eventually. That, to me, is a scary, scary world. But remember, we can shape what is normal with our choices. Why not shape it to goodness?

I'm not much of a gambler, as you will come to learn as you get older, but I will make a bet with you. I bet that at some point in your life you will be in some position of power. Whether at work, school, or volunteering—in some role, big or small. In some, if not all, of these positions, you will have an opportunity to abuse the power you have to enrich yourself at the expense of others; you will then have to decide whether to engage or not. This choice between goodness and power, between character and corruption, will have a real effect on other people's lives. It will affect what is normal. Because we came out of the state of nature and chose to live in communities, this tension between power and goodness, between corruption and integrity, will always be part of our lives. It's a struggle we have inherited from our mothers and fathers before us and their mothers and fathers before them. This may always be what mothers and fathers think as they prepare for their children to be born, but the America you are being born into seems more and more consumed by a lust for power and control, which leads to an ever-escalating cycle of conflict, rules, the struggle to control those rules, and more conflict.

I always wondered why your Dada wanted to sacrifice everything and move to the United States. One day, he finally told me. Part of what he sought was greater opportunities for prosperity, what he thought of as a better life, rather than the poverty he had experienced in his youth and early adulthood. But I will never forget what he told me next. He saw corruption in India, his motherland; and in America, his adoptive land. That is true. All places have some corruption, albeit in different forms. But your Dada believed the difference between corruption in India and America was that in America the corruption didn't affect "little people" in their everyday lives. Regular people could have a good life without having to succumb to the effects of corruption on a daily basis. In the halls of power, sure, there was corruption, but he respected that regular, everyday people didn't get squashed by it.

In the decades since I talked with your Dada, I have come to agree with him. Corruption leaches. It siphons prosperity through graft and rent seeking. It saps people of trust in each other and in institutions. It's a disease that slowly eats away at a pleasant, peaceful, and prosperous society. The real enemy of any society is not a policy decision or a rival faction—corruption is our common enemy. We all have a stake in solving the corruption problem.

My case for "why goodness" boils down to this: If we choose to live in community with others, corruption is inevitable. Accepting corruption is not an option—neither is homogenization. We can't depend on abundance to solve our problems, either. That leaves us with the choices of building institutions and character. But building more institutions comes at a hefty price because the more institutions we depend on, the less freedom we will have. Every rule we make constrains future choices. That leaves goodness as our best option, though building a society driven by goodness is challenging. If we choose to leave the state of nature and live in community with others, we must also choose the work and walk the path of goodness so that we can do our part to preserve as much of our freedoms as possible.

The world I hope for me and your mother, and the world I hope to pay forward to you, my three sons, is a world like the one renowned Bengali poet Rabindranath Tagore describes in "Gitanjali 35." Instead of succumbing to a culture struggling for power, I hope you aspire to find peace in goodness and that the world ends up requiring fewer rules and institutions as time goes on. I hope you are persuaded that our freedom, away from the ever-growing reach of rules and institutions, is inextricably linked to goodness. But for that to happen, more and more people must choose to walk the path of goodness, rather than power. And that my sons, starts with us and the choices we make every day of our lives. *We must choose.*

Love,
Your Papa

* * *

3

Abundance

In the real world, abundance isn't evenly distributed.

April 24, 2017

My Sons,

In our world, there isn't an unlimited supply of everything we want and need. We must deal with constraints and trade-offs, which cause stress, creating tension between what we want and what we have. That stress causes conflict. People act nutty when they are in scarcity; it makes them nutty in ways that make it even harder to get out of the scarcity they suffer from. For example, if you don't have enough money to feed your family, you might get stressed in ways that make you spend money more carelessly than you normally would. However, the scarcity I will speak about here is not just of food, water, and shelter, but of time, love, respect, or companionship—it includes scarcity of meaning.

How do you think the village in our thought experiment would be different if there wasn't scarcity? If the rule-enforcer in the tribe had enough, would he succumb to corruption as easily? If the prolific farmer wasn't worried that he might run out of food in the winter, would he be as willing to offer a corrupt proposition? Abundance, I suggest, is a way to mitigate corruption; people would have less need to cheat the system. Moreover, if abundance led to less conflict, there may be less need for "the system" to exist. But there's a reason I will write many letters about goodness in relation to power rather than abundance: it is because abundance doesn't solve the corruption problem; it merely displaces it. In the real world, abundance isn't evenly distributed. People are not perfectly just, nor do we have perfect institutions to mediate the distribution of gains from progress. After technology and other forms of progress create abundance, the surpluses are not evenly spread out.

Perhaps if we had an incredible level of abundance, where relative levels of scarcity between people were negligible, that would be sufficient to resolve the corruption problem. Then maybe we wouldn't have to struggle with becoming men who choose goodness. But that's not the world we live in, and we live in the most prosperous world in the history of humanity. We are not off the hook.

I felt I owed it to you to mention abundance more than just in passing, because it does matter. Now we have identified abundance as useful but not sufficient, let's return to our chief concerns: goodness and power. We have a lot to discuss.

Love,
Your Papa

* * *

4

What I Do and Do Not Mean

**This work is personal. It is self-improvement.
It is inner work. It is hard work.**

April 27, 2017

Boys,

Before going further, I want to clarify what we have covered so far. Here are things I expressly do not mean when I suggest you "choose the work" or "walk the path of goodness."

Choosing Good vs. Doing Good

In the world you are being born into, there seems to be a cultural movement to "do good," "make a positive change," or "make an impact," especially among millennials—my generation. Making a difference is vaunted as a life goal or career, and the benefits you bring to "the community" are used to demonstrate and measure that difference. For example, in my time living in Detroit, I have heard many people remark that they moved here so they could make a difference. Let's assume these people bring a benefit to the community that is more than self-serving. These are people I typify as "doing" good. Their deeds distinguish them from others. On the other hand, the way I typify people "choosing" good is how they make decisions, not what their decisions create. Their virtues and principles direct their choices at every moment and in every decision of their lives, related to the community or not. Doing is the what, choosing is the how.

To be sure, someone who consistently chooses good may also do good consistently and vice versa. I make this distinction because, in casual conversation, doing good and choosing good (i.e., being a good person) are often conflated as the same thing; they are not. You don't have to have a community-oriented job to be a good person. There are plenty of people who have jobs or side projects where they "do" good, but they are power-hungry and motivated by seeing their name in the paper—precisely the opposite of good in the way we are considering the topic. I am not concerned with exploring *doing* good, but rather, *choosing* good. I am concerned more about honing the process of how we act rather than the moral value of the outcomes of our actions. If we have a good process, a solid "how," if you will, the outcomes on balance will end up being good. If we focus on outcomes without working on our process for living, any good we "do" may simply be a coincidence. Again, both matter. I just want to be extremely clear about where I am choosing to focus.

Happiness vs. Goodness

You may be tempted to think an adequate proxy for goodness is figuring out what makes you feel happy and pursuing that. Or, figuring out what makes other people happy and pursuing that. That is not what I mean. The pursuit of goodness and the pursuit of happiness are not interchangeable. Of course, some pursuits of happiness are also pursuits of goodness. For example, I feel happy when I tell the truth, go on hikes in the woods, complete my chores, or spend time with family. Similarly, there are actions that are not pursuits of happiness or of goodness either, like torturing animals, cursing someone out, or stealing money. If we stopped here, it would be plausible to think that *goodness = happiness* and *not goodness = not happiness*. But alas, there are plenty of pursuits of happiness that are not of goodness, like getting rip-roaring drunk.

Drinking to drunkenness put me in an energetic and happy mood many a time. Ripping a shot at a party, then dancing to anthems like Whitney Houston's *I Wanna Dance with Somebody* with best friends on a Monday night at Rick's American Café (my favorite college bar) is great! But those times I have been drunk haven't always been consistent with goodness. There were times I was a happy drunk but also a jackass. I once sloppily asked a girl out on a date around a bunch of friends at a bar and was loud and obnoxious when she politely refused. I was in a happy mood because I was drunk, but I was a jackass. Again, happiness isn't a proxy for goodness; in fact, sometimes what makes us feel unhappy is what helps us grow to be better.

When I was a consultant traveling to different parts of the country to work on projects, I went to some awesome places: Salt Lake City, Chicago, Napa Valley, and San Francisco were probably my favorites. But I also went to a few places I would have never gone to otherwise, like Western Kentucky. When I received the assignment, I was not happy about going. I went because my client had a factory there. They made laundry detergent. I was working on a project related to warehouses for that laundry detergent, so I went to talk to the people who worked in the warehouse. So, there I was, in a town in Kentucky so small I can't remember what it was called. At the time and to this day, the people I knew, the articles I read, and television newscasts I watched made me assume that Western Kentucky was full of angry, country bumpkin people who were backwards and probably racist. When I found out I was going to Kentucky, I was worried. Would people treat me poorly when I arrived? Would I face physical intimidation? When I got there, I was nervous and had a big chip on my shoulder.

Yet, what people were actually like in Kentucky was so different than I expected. It was a town with the friendliest people I have ever met in any of my work travels; they were also hardworking, smart, and kind. They were not racist, to me at least, and I couldn't picture anyone I met (of any race) being hurtful to anyone. Because of what I had heard about Western Kentucky, it would have been rational for me to behave badly, boss people around, or act rudely and arrogantly. I'm glad I didn't act on my preconceived notions. That experience in Western Kentucky taught me important lessons: there is good in most people; people may surprise you; and if you give people the chance to be kind or succeed, they often meet the moment. My trip to the detergent warehouse was not initially a pursuit of happiness; more than anything, it was a professional obligation, but that pursuit ended up changing my perspective and making me a better man.

Hence, pursuing happiness and pursuing goodness are not the same thing. Happiness has its place, but it's not the idea I care about discussing in these letters.

Goodness: A Working Definition

I can't give you a cut-and-dry definition for goodness. Or a checklist or formula. Goodness is something I had to discover on my own. Understanding all that goodness is will take me a lifetime. Again, I will do my best to share what I have learned so you can make more useful mistakes than I have.

Let's go back to the village, where delegating power to a rule-enforcer was necessary to ensure the rules were followed. That is a problematic strategy because the second you give someone power, that person becomes vulnerable to corruption. So, there were basic solutions to dealing with corruption after moving past the unviable options of homogenization and abundance: building institutions and character. Let me use that construct as a litmus test for "goodness."

As we make choices, they affect the world and culture around us. What effect are we having? Do our choices make the world need more or fewer institutions? If a choice you make allows society to move toward more trust and less institutions and rules, you are probably acting with goodness. If a choice you make moves society further away from trust and it needs more institutions and rules, you are probably not acting with goodness.

My thinking here is that, in an idyllic situation, everyone is perfectly good. In that case, we would never need rules, rule-enforcers, or government because we would be able to handle conflict without them, if we had conflict at all. So, if our actions move us closer to that ideal state, it is probably a good sign that our actions would be considered "good."

Of course, that is not a perfect definition. It's serviceable at best, and there are many complicating factors and degrees of impact. But the question—would the action I am taking require our world to have more rules in the long run, or fewer?—does get us somewhere.

The Work

I have said to you, "I hope you choose the work," but what does that mean? What is the choice? What is *the work*? The choice is the one presented in *East of Eden* when Sam Hamilton, Lee, and Adam Trask are discussing *timshel*, "thou mayest." We, as mortals, grapple with the idyllic good and the messy evil that can take hold of us and the world around us. But we can choose to conquer sin and find redemption; we can choose good over evil. But that greatest of all choices comes at a cost: it takes *work*. When we choose to walk the path of goodness, we are also choosing the work that comes with it. This work is not a school reading assignment or manual labor. It is not "work" in the way I go to work to earn money to buy bread. This work is personal. It is self-improvement. It is inner work. It is hard work.

The hardest part of writing these letters to you is grasping what the work is. There is, after all, no owner's manual for the work of slowly purifying a man's soul. This book describes how I think it can work. It contains a logic model and is the operating system for how I live my life.

The first hurdle is that, when we are born, we don't know

who we are and how we aspire to be. We must figure this out. We must answer questions like: *What is good? What is having a purer soul? What could that be like?* Ultimately, we have the hardest question in this line of inquiry: *Am I a good person?* My sons, that is not a natural question to answer because we know we are not perfect. We know we are not finished and still have work to do. *Am I a good person?* is a difficult question to answer honestly, but more importantly, it's a difficult one to bring ourselves *to ask.* To ask a question that consequential requires an insatiable curiosity. That is our first area of focus when we choose the work: we must develop a strong muscle of curiosity so we can even bring ourselves to ask the question. If we ask that question, and answer honestly, we find we are not finished works, that we can be more good than we are. To become more good, there may be some easy habits to break, but by and large, modifying beliefs and behaviors, that will really make a difference in helping us to be better, will be hard. And when I say hard, I mean *really damn hard.* To be better men, we must face our deepest fears, ask forgiveness from those we have wronged, and rewrite our most destructive and demeaning habits.

Our next area of work is to develop a strong muscle of courage; we need to see the hard actions ahead of us and do them despite knowing they are hard and do them repeatedly, in perpetuity, not just once. And so, the final area of work is to develop a strong muscle of persistence because, to become better, we need the stamina to do hard stuff repeatedly.

Good vs. Perfect

The stakes of making the great choice are enormous; not only is our culture in the balance, but also our souls. I am not saying you need to be perfect or the best. I want that to be crystal clear. The pressure to be perfect, to never make mistakes, has long held my inner self in bondage. It has slunk over and suffocated my psyche. I spent much of my life in self-flagellation, hurting my own feelings before anyone else could, punishing myself because that was what I thought I deserved. Anything short of perfection was a failure. No. No. No. No. NO. The point of the great choice and choosing the work is not to become a perfect being. We are not gods. If you try to be perfect, you will surely fail and eventually descend into depression, madness, or both. The point of choosing the work is to *do* the work.

You may be thinking, *my father wrote to his sons about goodness, and now he is saying he doesn't think the point is to actually be good?* My sons, I believe that if you make your focus the work, and if you consciously choose that work and put your whole effort into it, you will become the men you were meant to be. You will indeed become good men. Focus on the work itself, with zeal. As my high school junior varsity football coaches taught me, "Let the wins and losses take care of themselves." Try to become a slightly better man every day. Do not walk the path of goodness to become perfect. There is no guarantee you will become what other people say is a good man. The glory of life is not to receive the world's recognition or the applause of men.

—

I love you boys fiercely and deeply, but also desperately. My

43

fatherly heart is so deeply invested in you, I think about your happiness, your peace, and the men you will someday become. Even at this young age, the slightest bit of pain you feel is a dagger to my abdomen. I want you all to be happy, to have peace, to be good men, for when one has happiness, peace, and integrity, joy often follows.

Though my heart longs so strongly for these things, my better angels prevail. More than anything, my sons, I want to help you to be yourselves, to be honest and kind. I have faith that if you choose the work, you will find life's great glories. I have faith that when you end your journey of this life, you will find yourself in a good place, where you are meant to be.

You are smart, thoughtful, hardworking men—I see this already. And yet, despite how smart, thoughtful, and hardworking you are, there will still be many aspects of the world you cannot control. And the work, no matter how smart and committed you are, will be difficult. My hope is that I can give you a place to start and stack the odds just a bit more in your favor. I hope that your biggest takeaway, too, is not the lessons from the words I write, but that you see this book as an enduring reminder that I have, do, and will always love you unconditionally. I will tell you what I have figured out, and you three can figure out what I could not.

I've been thinking about this for years now, but this journey truly began generations ago. What you will learn is based on what your mom and I learned from your grandparents. And what your grandparents learned is based on what they learned from their parents before them. And back like this for generations. What I am sharing with you has little to do with just your mom and I; it is wisdom that has been waiting generations for you. Someday, you too will pass on this torch that connects generations.

Love,
Papa

* * *

5

Curiosity

Learn something new; do something special.

May 7, 2017

Boys,

Curiosity is like water to me. I can't remember a time I wasn't curious. When I learn something new, or explore an idea by reading or asking someone a question who has more expertise than me, I get a gleeful satisfaction. Sometimes, tapping into a new idea makes my skin tingle. In a way, discovering something new is a relief, like icy cold water hitting a parched tongue. It's exciting, like finding a secret passageway. Or coming across a distant cairn on a difficult trail, signaling you are one step closer to knowing the truth. It's a feeling of connecting to millions of people, both alive and gone ahead, who learned what you learned and explored the idea you are exploring.

These days, learning something new mostly makes me feel echoes of your Dada. To him, learning was such a delight.

He insisted upon it and brought tremendous intensity to it. Learning was when he was freest and most himself. He passed that exhilaration for learning to me, and I to you. There was no way for us not to. Writing this letter to you about curiosity reminds me of his sincerity, warmth, and honesty. I miss him and hope sharing these thoughts on curiosity is something he would be proud of.

Learning is a special craft for your granddad, too. When your mother and her siblings were growing up, he would say, "learn something new; do something special" before every school day, every day. But I'll let your mother tell you more about that. It's a special memory of hers.

Let's turn to curiosity and why it is work we must do. Let's say you want to become a great cook. So, you decide to cook something. You have seen your mother and I make meals at home, so you know at least something about cooking: some of the smells, that burnt food tastes bad, food flavor combinations you like... Since you don't have much experience, you begin your adventure with a simple family favorite: macaroni and cheese. If what you know about macaroni and cheese is based on what you've eaten before, where do you begin? Where do you get ingredients? You would have to know how to grocery shop. You would have to know something about cheeses and pasta and which to choose. Once you have bought ingredients, you would have to know how to operate a stove, which pots and pans to use, and how much macaroni to combine with how much cheese. All that for a simple dish! Cooking requires much more contextual knowledge than what a recipe contains.

When you have figured out how to make macaroni and cheese, and you will, you can't consider yourself a *great* cook because the dish is not that complicated, nor nutritious. To be a better cook, you must learn more dishes and fundamental preparation techniques like boiling, sautéing, and kneading. You must learn more about the stove, oven, knives, and other tools. You must learn to use your senses. After that, you could be a decent cook. But a great one? Achieving mastery requires another level of learning. Great cooks know more than just how to prepare a dish, they know that the sogginess that comes after putting salt into the *gobi* is chemistry. They know the kneading motion to give the boule shape is a lesson in proteins. They know a hot pan cracking when doused with ice water is not voodoo, but physics. They understand that food affects health and is also history, culture, customs, and tradition. They understand something about art and design and are particular about how food is presented. Great cooks know about operations concepts like *mise en place*.

To be a great cook, there is much to learn—not just related to the most obvious elements of cooking, but across many disciplines and traditions. It is hard work and certainly does not happen overnight. *The work* functions in the same way. You must learn many truths from peripheral disciplines. You start with the basics and practice, and it takes years of discipline to get there. You won't be paid or compensated for your efforts, just like cooking in our home kitchen. So why would anyone want to learn to be a great cook, and not for pay? After all, it's quite a commitment with few tangible rewards. That raises a fundamental question: What motivates someone to learn and be better? If we can answer this, we will know something about what may motivate someone to choose the work, too.

There is a concept from the social sciences that is helpful here: intrinsic and extrinsic motivation. Intrinsic motivation comes from the happiness, joy, or meaning you get from a task. Extrinsic motivation, on the other hand, comes from earning a reward or benefit from the external world. With the work, there is no extrinsic reward coming. There is no certificate nor medal for learning to do the right thing. Let's assume the saying "good things happen to good people" is true; that's hardly an effective extrinsic motivator because the time between when we do a good deed, and when we receive the reward, is so long, it's not in our minds when we're learning. We can't depend on extrinsic factors to motivate us to be good people. When it comes to learning how to cook, or learning to be good people, we have no choice but to draw from intrinsic motivation. We must find pleasure or interest in the act of learning itself, especially when exploring difficult ideas like goodness, which requires learning across multiple topics.

Curiosity is the self-motivating desire to learn. If we want to learn for learning's sake, we must be curious. If we are curious, we want to learn for learning's sake. That's what curiosity *is*. Curiosity creates a gentle but exciting tension within us that is satiated by learning, which makes learning pleasurable. Just like a joke cannot have a funny punchline without a setup, learning cannot create intrinsic satisfaction without curiosity. Just like the Temptation and the Hawaiian War Chant, you cannot have one without the other (you'll get that joke later in life, it's a University of Michigan Marching Band reference). That is why curiosity is the first critical capability of the work. Without it, there is no foundation for the intrinsic motivation needed to learn on your own and, in turn, discover what goodness is over the course of your lifetime. Because goodness offers little extrinsic reward, we must depend on curiosity and the willingness to learn to motivate our pursuit of goodness.

I hope you are curious about this world and how it works. I hope you are curious about the solar system, the universe, God, history, music, politics, psychology, management, chemistry, physics, mathematics, and so many other things. I hope you explore people, places, planets, and philosophies beyond your own. I wish you a life of voracious learning and discovery. If we choose the work, we need to know the truth, not just about the world around us, but also the truth about ourselves. Self-examination is crucial.

By now, I hope the question you're asking is, *well Papa, how do I become curious?* All the best ideas, stories, and learnings I have had are about how to cultivate and nurture the curiosity within us, so we can become curious about the world around us, and in the quality of our own character. I'm excited to talk about it with you all as you learn to talk and think.

Love,
Your Papa

* * *

6

Slow Down

**To be curious,
we have to slow down.**

May 27, 2017

My Sons,

The most important class I took in business school was not a traditional MBA course. It was a practicum and had three components: (1) launching a business using the lean startup method; (2) working with an executive coach; and (3) working with Dr. Melissa Peet on exercises related to a field she is pioneering called Generative Knowledge. To start off one of our sessions, Dr. Peet had us do a simple exercise, which turned out to be incredibly insightful, despite its modesty. The exercise is in three parts and requires a large room. If you are in a large room, try it out as we go.

First, walk around the room like you are in "problem-solving mode." Silently, walk and act as if you are trying to fix something, or as if you are working on a serious group project

51

at school. Spend about a minute projecting a problem-solving mindset. Now that you have done it, what did you notice about the room? How did your body feel? What were you thinking about? What were you doing with your limbs?

Next, walk around the room for another minute or two and pretend you are in "social mode"—relaxing, hanging out with friends, or taking a walk for fun. Ask yourself the same questions. How did it feel?

Finally, walk around the room and push yourself to be like someone who is *radically* curious. After you're done, ask yourself the same questions. While reflecting, add one more question: What was different about each round of the exercise?

You probably felt very different at each stage of the exercise, mentally and physically. One of the biggest changes you probably noticed between the three rounds was speed: of your walking, of your heart rate, of your mind. When you walk in problem-solving mode, everything is fast. It's the pace of "getting stuff done." Social mode is not as fast, but it is faster than the mode of radical curiosity. When your head space is not just curious, but *radically curious*, everything slows down. Radical curiosity is intense, but slow.

The lesson is obvious: *to be curious we have to slow down*. In order to learn, your mind, body, and heart need to be open and absorbent, and that requires slowing down. In this world you were born into, slowing down is hard. You will be trained, cajoled, and incentivized—anything to get you to go fast. To have any shot at curiosity and mental clarity, you *must not* acquiesce. So many people I have met are obsessed with "getting things done," doing more with less, hustling, and the like. It's practically a national obsession to want to maximize time and effort, and squeeze in as many bucket list items and experiences as you can. Be cautious, my sons, it is a trap, one I will show you how to avoid. It is a trap I was in for the first 28 years of my life. If you become too busy, it will be difficult to develop radical curiosity, which will make it difficult to choose the work and ultimately to pursue goodness.

Practice slowing down. Your mother and I have tried to do this. It's hard, especially because we are both problem solvers (read: we are crazy people), we have had periods of obsession with job success, and we are social. I'm not saying to leave problems unsolved or to be antisocial, and there is, of course, a time and place to move fast. The mistake I see a lot of people making, and that I've made a lot, is never slowing down. Because you will inherit some of our genes and habits, you will probably have a hard time slowing down, too. Here are some of the techniques I have tried, which I hope work for you. Remember, slowing down is learned behavior and a blessing.

1. Get Outside

The easiest way I know to slow down is to get outside: in the sun, rain, heat or cold, it doesn't matter. Nature isn't constrained by petty human concerns; it moves at its own pace. Take a walk outside just to walk. Being in nature is restorative, and fortunately, slow. I didn't realize this until my first camping trip with Uncle Jeff and Uncle Ellis a few months after I graduated college. We were in the High Peaks region of the Adirondack Mountains. I had no idea what I was doing, and they were my guides.

There's a moment I distinctly remember during that adventure, probably about 20-30 minutes into our hike, something I had never experienced before: *quiet*—no cars or ambient noise coming from machines or civilization.

As I write this letter to you, I am sitting on the couch in the family room, in one of the quietest neighborhoods in the city, before 9a.m., on a Saturday, on a holiday weekend. Your mom and Riley are sleeping, but I still hear noises: the occasional car passing by; the dull hum of the refrigerator; the electronics equipment that is always on. Every day has some human-produced noise. Those noises handcuff us to problem-solving mode or social mode; they hijack our attention. Whether deep in the backcountry, relatively untouched by humans, or in a park in the middle of a city (like Belle Isle or Central Park in New York), or just the sidewalk of our neighborhood on a sleepy Saturday morning, getting outside will help you slow down and open up to the curiosity mindset.

2. Schedule Unscheduled Time

Before your mother and I were married, one challenge we had to overcome was burning ourselves out by overscheduling our lives. We were rarely relaxed. All our time was scheduled "fast time": dinner; socializing; volunteering; working—and we couldn't set the pace. We decided we needed to schedule fewer things, so we left our calendar open more. That approach quickly failed because last-minute plans tended to come up a lot, especially when you were young. When plans sound like fun, and you like who proposed them, and your calendar isn't full, it's easy to say yes. I'm that way: last minute plans are like potato chips to me; I can't turn them down, even though I know they will make me sluggish the next day. So we actively scheduled "slow time" instead of keeping the calendar free, and started a simple practice we called "Black-out Day." We blacked out our calendar by picking one night a week to have no plans. It helped. Slow time is not a time to "catch-up" on work or e-mails, or to be "productive," but to rest and decompress.

If you need to do something, let it be creative. Write. Bake. Paint. Talk to family. Sing. Meditate (it is a remarkable antidote to fast living). Find something and stick with it.

3. Take Real Vacations

If you read this while you are still in middle or high school, you may think this is obvious, but it's not. Taking a real vacation is not easy. Work and ambition get in the way. When I was a management consultant, I had a surprising amount of vacation days—about 25 days in a year—but often, I wouldn't use them. That's step one. You have to prioritize vacation enough to actually take it. When you are working, there will be times you will think you cannot take a vacation. This probably means you are trapped in thinking that your work is more important than your health, your life, and your family. Or, you haven't prepared your team well enough to function without you.

When you are on vacation, you must stop working, *actually be there*. Leave your computer at home if you can. Don't check your messages and communication tools. That is one reason I like to vacation in nature, in a national park: it's often impossible to be reached.

Vacations help clear your mind. Remember, those days off are part of your employment contract, so use them. You are giving money away if you don't. In recent years, I have tried to apply this thinking to any day off, including weekends. Weekends, in a way, are two-day vacations you get every week.

When your mom and I look back at our childhoods, we fondly remember the vacations we took with our families. For your mom, it was trips she took to Myrtle Beach or up north. For me, it was going to India, Orlando, or New York. We both remember trips to Disney. Those trips were the uninterrupted times we had with our families, where deep relationships and bonds were formed, and are the ones your mom and I can't wait to have with you and the rest of our family and friends.

Life is beautiful, but it goes fast. Slow it down however you can.

Love,
Your Papa

* * *

7

Read

Curiosity must be nurtured, lest it stop.

May 28, 2017

My Sons,

The first week your mother and I moved into this house, we asked each other what our favorite room was. We both said, "the library." You have been born into a family of bookworms.

Reading is an emotional release, a vacation, a time machine. The best books are great art. Masterful stories take you around the world, the universe, and into fantasy. They take you into joyous moments of a character's life, or make you feel terrible feelings safely.

Growing up, your Dada and Dadi read with me and would take me to the library all the time, wherever we lived. There are cassette tapes of us reading together, which I cherish. I've received many books as gifts from your mom, aunts, uncles, and grandparents that remind me of the tremendous love and care I am blessed to have. The best discussions I have had come from reading books. They have made my life so much richer. Beyond this, there are many practical benefits, especially related to becoming curious and doing the work. Reading needs no practical purpose to justify it; more than anything, I think you should read because it is beautiful.

To become curious, reading is essential. But I don't mean read as in casually thumbing through some rubbish while you watch television. To develop curiosity, you must *really* read. With intention, oomph, with some measure of patience, presence, and the desire to absorb the densely packed nourishment the author is offering. Reading a good book or essay is serious soul food; it is to digest a potent, concentrated morsel of insight.

Writing, too, is much like making a sauce in that sense, a sauce with delicious ingredients: water; wine; cream; herbs, spices. When making a sauce, the chef must take great care so the excess liquid is evaporated away and the sauce thickens. What remains is concentrated and flavorful, with a better texture. A good writer evaporates the unnecessary, leaving only the ideas that are aromatic, flavorful, and potent. Consequently, reading great works is an efficient medium for cultivating curiosity and leaves you hungrier than when you started.

Writing is a great labor in service to you, the reader, but, as a reader, you have a tremendous labor of your own. There's a difference between reading and *really reading.* The first litmus test between reading and *really reading* is that of purpose: Are you reading for comprehension, for the pages, or to learn? Reading for comprehension implies you are reading to remember what the author is saying, to understand the basic who, what, where, when, and why. You are not reading for deeper thought or for a nuanced understanding of the idea or story. In these circumstances, you just want to put information into your head and recall it coherently. Reading for the pages, on the other hand, is something to avoid. It's not worth your time; it probably means you are cutting corners, or worse, reading to feign intelligence (which, at its root, is a power-seeking behavior). You are reading to finish the book or essay as fast as possible and "get it done." The goal of reading for the pages is less about gaining something from the text, but more about being able to tell other people you have read it. Reading to learn is an entirely different enterprise. The intended outcome is not just literally understanding what the author is saying. Rather, it is to change yourself in some way, whether that is deepening your understanding of an idea, seeing the world in a new way, or changing your mind about something. If something about you, however small, is not changed, you have not learned. Reading to learn takes tremendous focus. You must listen to the author and focus. That means eliminating all distractions and ignoring the concerns of your day-to-day life for a while. The book must be your only concern because we mortal men tend to not be good at multitasking. It is also best, in my experience, to read slowly (your mother is good at this; if you watch her read, you can tell by the way she moves her eyes that she is methodical and incisive). Reading slowly allows you to not only absorb and comprehend what the author is saying, but to also question it—even explore it through a daydream. When reading slowly, you create the opportunity to reflect on what you are reading and ask questions like:

- Why?

- Is that believable?
- Why would the author mention that?
- What is the author not saying?
- How does this relate to the overall thesis of the book?
- Why did the author use this particular word?
- How is the author biased?
- What works has the author built upon?
- How could I build on this idea?
- How does this idea play out in real life?
- How does what the author is saying affect my life?

You cannot ask these important, inward-changing questions, let alone reflect on them, if you do not go slowly. Moreover, deeply emotional books, or those rich with ideas and provocative arguments, aren't always easy to read. They take time. You may have to read passages again and again or the book in its entirety. (I have re-read *Profiles in Courage*, the *Bhagavad Gita*, and *East of Eden*.)

What you read matters. As I've learned from working on technology and data projects, "garbage in, garbage out." What you put into your mind will affect what comes out of it. I'm not suggesting that you only read dense, esoteric, nerdy books from a limited list of "appropriate" subjects. On the contrary, I think you should read whatever you like (though I highly suggest a mix of fiction and non-fiction; I spent many years avoiding fiction, but it's wonderful and transformative to read both) and mix subjects and genres between ones you are already interested in and ones that expand your mind. For example, I'm currently pawing through a short story collection gifted to me years ago by Miss Emily, a friend of mine from high school. It is Russian literature from the 1800s and a remarkably illuminating, relevant read, with prose that leaves me arrested and whimsical at the same time.

But there are also *terrible* books, where it is plain the author did not develop an original, valuable thought, or produce clear, deliberate, enchanting prose. Terrible is less about topic and more about quality and honesty. There are books that are well written but are intellectually dishonest, biased, or tell you what you already believe solely for commercial purposes. These are terrible and dangerous because they teach what is untrue or immoral.

For many years, I made the mistake of reading a narrow set of topics, usually business or government. Or, I read books I was more interested in telling people I was reading, rather than what I was interested in reading (those were usually about business and government, too). This was "reading for the pages" because the books I chose were driven by the expectations of others, rather than my own desires. Do not fear reading about a wide set of topics. If you read a quality book, it will stay with you and enrich your life and the lives of others around you, regardless of the topic. More often than not, reading across disciplines will give you a mental model that helps you make sense of a difficult idea in your primary area of interest. Intellectual diversity is important. There's no better person to explain why diversity matters than Scott Page, one of the professors I was lucky to have during my undergraduate studies. We have a few of the books he's written on our bookshelves at home.

Your Aunt Lyssi gave me a book last Christmas that uses computer science concepts to show how humans make decisions. It is brilliant and has helped me to make sense of how we organize the cookware in our kitchen and how to conduct a search to fill a job at work. The idea of a cache was the concept helpful in the kitchen: items we don't use often should go in the cupboard instead of on the counter. There's also an algorithm for optimal stopping that's useful to keep in mind when filling a position. The book, *Algorithms to Live By*, is on our bookshelf, too. You will probably notice I have often told you about reading books, as opposed to reading blogs, newspapers, magazines, or anything else. I've started to shy away from those except for blogs, local newspapers, and *The Economist*. I think blogs are great because they occupy niches and go deep into a topic rather than appealing to a mass audience. I have cycled through many authors and subjects over the years, like interstellar travel, data visualization, marketing, strategy, personal memories, grief, and others. I like *The Economist* because it has a unique perspective: it's globally focused and comes out weekly, so it's not chasing stories frivolously, and it's hilariously cheeky. Most daily publications, I have found, mix in fluff stories to get clicks and have bombastic headlines to get attention. *The Economist* avoids this. Also, there's a simple reason for my emphasis on books. I've found that the quality of a piece of writing is inversely proportional to how hard it is to write and how long it takes to write. In that way, daily publications are often low quality. If the publication is covering yesterday's news, the writer can only put a few hours of work into it. There are exceptions, but I've come to prefer books.

What does this all have to do with curiosity and choosing goodness? When I was growing up, personal computing was emerging, as was the Internet. One of the antecedents of this idea is thinking of the mind as a computer and describing the functions of the brain as functions of a computer's component parts. However, I have come to see the brain as much more than a biological information-processing machine. The scientific consensus seems to be that we know very little about the brain, consciousness, and the mind. This will probably change a lot during your lifetime, and that's exciting. The mind, that which creates new ideas and is susceptible to inspiration and wonder, is not fixed or static. It evolves.

Curiosity, that voracious appetite, causes the mind to grow and evolve. Curiosity must be nurtured, lest it stop. Without curiosity, the mind becomes more like a machine. In that way, curiosity is foundational to keeping us human: it inoculates the mind from becoming stiff and like a machine. *Really* reading nourishes curiosity. When you take a good book and really read it, it forces you to pay attention and consider new possibilities. It forces your mind to work in ways it hasn't before and stay flexible. Really reading does more than simply adding information to your memory bank: it keeps your mind from *becoming* a memory bank. It also cultivates curiosity because of how much ground you can cover in a book. Books transcend time, space, and reality quickly. Books don't replace real-life experiences, but in books you can try things out. You can expose yourself to different circumstances and ideas, which allows your mind to consider different questions and perspectives. Reading a book leaves you wanting more, which leads to more reading, which leads to more learning, which leads to wanting more, and so on.

In your daily life, nobody will make you reflect on goodness or how to choose the work it requires with consistency. The country you are being born into has a sophisticated structure of laws, institutions, and incentives—none of which specifically encourage or reward goodness or good character, and some are simply designed with other intentions as their primary concern. Our institutions depend on being able to measure things so they can be managed; this is hard to do with goodness. It can take a lifetime to begin to grasp goodness and choose it consistently. If goodness is hard to even define, how can it be measured, managed, codified, prioritized, and incentivized? This, again, is why I want to share these letters with you and try to share in them some of the traits and tools I've found helpful, in hopes that they will help you figure out how to consistently choose goodness over the course of your lifetime.

A good book, my sons, is a wise, honest friend that pushes you to consider the most difficult questions asked of human beings. They can be fearless in ways we cannot be because they do not die, which allows their truths to be timeless and immortal. Plato, John Steinbeck, Jhumpa Lahiri, George Orwell, Marilynne Robinson, Peter Drucker, President John F. Kennedy—men and women I have never met—have pushed me to think about the world, about goodness, justice, courage, and my own identity and existence in profound ways. They are people, through their writing, who have—with the greatest care and love—compelled me to endure the interrogation of gravely important questions in a way that only compares to the people who love me most in the world. Books are superhuman because of their ability to make those who *really* read them consider the topics and questions humans struggle to raise with each other.

The happiest memories of my childhood are the times I read with your Dada and Dadi. These memories, some of my earliest, are ones I've thought of often since your Dada went ahead last year. I've been trying to hold on to them as long as

I can.

So, I promise I will help you to love reading, just as your Dada and Dadi did for me and your Mimi and Granddad did for your mother. I cannot wait to read with you. Your mother and I have already talked about how eager we are to bring you into the worlds of *Harry Potter, The Lord of the Rings*, and *The Phantom Tollbooth.* I feel like I have been waiting my whole life to read these stories to you, one night, one chapter at a time.

Loving to really read is so much bigger than just you and me. Reading is more than getting good grades in school or entertainment. Once you really read a good book, it gives you another ally on your journey, to work toward goodness. And that's what matters most.

Love,
Your Papa

* * *

8

Ask Simple Questions

These questions are not just part of the work:
they are the work.

July 2, 2017

My Sons,

In my last letter to you, I shared my honest reflections on how to *really* read. Books develop and satiate curiosity, which is the first pillar of the work. But there is much more out there to explore than what you find in books. Other people are out there too, and within them are centuries of life experience. With every person you meet, comes their unique, beautiful, and complex inner world.

People and their meditations about their experiences are rich sources of the stuff that cultivates curiosity. Many wonderful thoughts, stories, and ideas never make it into books. These thoughts remain exactly that—thoughts—until they are discussed in open air. This, to me, is what is special about conversations. Potent thoughts are unleashed, and wisdom is shared with others.

How does one unleash wisdom residing in the minds of others? Ask questions. However simple that may seem, there is much to consider about questions: how to ask them; what to ask about; how to listen. Let's explore why questions are critical to cultivating curiosity and how to ask them well.

Foremost, ask lots of questions. Quantity drives quality. The more sincere questions you ask, the better you will become at asking them. The worst question is the one never asked; the second worst is the question you don't actually care to know the answer to.

When you are learning something new, your questions will be novice and unsophisticated. You may feel shy about asking a specific question. That doesn't matter. If you sincerely want to know, ask the question. I promise, as you ask more questions, the easier it will get and the more fruitful they will become. Like most things, asking questions takes practice. The best way to get better is to just ask more questions. If you're going through the trouble of asking questions in the first place, you might as well ask good ones. The best advice I can give you is three-fold: be simple; be sincere; and follow-up.

In 2015, I took a great class with Bob Quinn during my last semester in business school called Transformational Leadership. It changed my life. We read two of Professor Quinn's books: *Lift* and *Deep Change*. *Lift*'s framework is brilliant: when doing something new, ask yourself the four Lift questions. The first, and most important, is: "What result are we trying to create?" When asking that question and the three others, you become focused, grounded, and motivated. In class, we put the concepts of *Lift* into practice. I asked myself the four Lift questions about how I use Facebook. I came up with an idea to ask a sincere, reflective question every day on Facebook. I no longer ask a question every day, but I do it several times a week. Asking these questions has helped me to learn greatly about the hopes, dreams, and beliefs of others and myself. I understand the human condition better now due to asking questions openly and transparently on Facebook. Beyond that, I likely have nearly 1,000 reps asking questions. That's rich data that has helped me to understand how to ask a good question.

The best questions are simple, which means they are clear, succinct, and written in plain language. Every word has a purpose. There is no fluff. A good rule of thumb is to be able to ask a question in one breath, in one short sentence. Asking questions in this way makes them easier to answer. People appreciate simple questions and, in my experience, tend to answer them with greater energy, detail, and honesty.

My college friend, Ms. Lainie, received advice from her mother that I always thought was smart and charming: *If you really want a man to understand what they are supposed to do, you have to be able to write your direction on one side of one Post-it note. If not, it's too complicated.* She shared it in the context of a wife giving her husband a task to do, but I think it also applies to questions. If you hold yourself to the standard of asking a simple question, and practice doing so, you start to get choosy about words and framing. If a question is short, each word matters more and is more likely to reframe the question's meaning. Choosing words carefully makes your question more specific, which makes the answers you receive to them richer and more relevant. The simpler the question, the better.

In asking hundreds and thousands of questions on Facebook, I have also realized I get better, clearer, and more interesting responses when I ask sincerely—when I ask questions I really want to know the answer to or that I'm genuinely curious about. I don't have data and studies to back this up, but other people don't trust you when they think you don't really care about the answer, if you're trying to brag, or if you're trying to trap them with their answers. They can tell. It's hard to fake sincerity in the long run. People just have a feel for it.

Lots of people ask questions they either already know the answer to, or don't *really* want to know the answers to. For us then, the advice is simple. If you really want to know the answer to a question, ask it. If you don't, don't.

Another way to ask a good question is to follow it up with another question, and another, and maybe a few more. To truly learn, you must dig deep. Treasure is normally buried more than six inches below the surface. A well-crafted question, sincerely asked, begets learning, which begets curiosity, which begets even more well-crafted questions. If you ask good questions, it starts a vigorous cycle of learning and curiosity. So, be simple, be sincere, and follow-up.

There are certainly more questions you can add to your repertoire, but here are a few of mine that are tried and true that apply to many situations:

- What result are we trying to create? Why?
- What's that?
- How does that work?
- Why do we do it this way?
- Who is this for?
- What do you think?
- What happened, exactly?
- How do you feel about this?

- Why does this matter to you?

In addition to asking questions of others, it is essential that you ask questions of yourself—you must reflect. Questioning yourself is not a trivial activity. Even if you have managed to muster the humility to acknowledge the fallibility of your own character and question it, you must then do something even harder: be honest answering your questions, as they are great tools to determine what goodness is and whether you are actually embodying it—questions such as: What does a good person think and do? And am I a good person? This inquiry is a true test of whether you are motivated to endure the lifelong struggle of developing your character. Remember, questions wielded irresponsibly can be an instrument of power and control. Leading questions help you to hear the answer you want to hear, instead of the truth. Questions can be asked in a way that raises false hearsay or bullies others with shame instead of pushing toward truth. It is up to you to use questions with good intent. This takes effort and practice.

In my life, I have been taught how to reflect—and I am better for it. It started because of a lucky break in school. I was always part of the student council and student groups. Because of my involvement, I attended conferences and camps designed to develop leadership in youth. Student Council Camp likely changed the course of my life because the adults there made reflection a foundational part of the curriculum. Real learning occurred during the debriefs that occurred after activities were complete. The counselors pushed us to articulate our thoughts and feelings by asking introspective questions regarding identity, integrity, justice, and conflict. They would dig and dig and then ask why again. I have tremendous gratitude for the student council advisers and camp counselors I had in high school because they taught me to reflect on my actions and thoughts. They challenged me to be honest with myself about whether I was a good person with true character. It is now my responsibility to help you. Ask your mother, too, about Kairos—a retreat she went on in high school. I think you will find it's an experience that affected her in a similar way.

No matter what, when it comes to reflection, you just have to start somewhere. (I have always liked to reflect through writing.) Your mom and I started to talk and reflect together when we started dating. We would do a "temperature check" every week on Sundays, taking turns answering the same five questions: What do you appreciate about your partner? What are your issues? What are your requests for change? What are you thinking about outside of the relationship? What are the logistics of the week? Your mother and I continue this practice to this day, and we have missed less than one weekly temperature check a year in our whole relationship.

I am not trying to prescribe a reflection mechanism for you, I am merely offering suggestions. You must create protected time, with a clear mind, to slow down and step away from the challenges of day-to-day life. You might even need a dedicated, regular physical space for reflection, whether it's a notebook, a place in the house, a hideaway around the city, or in nature. Perhaps the most difficult space to come by is in your heart. When you first open your heart, humbly, to reflect, it will be uncomfortable. It will be uncomfortable to ask yourself tough questions because you may not like what you discover. When I was having drinks with Brendan (Uncle B) and his friend Zack over Thanksgiving this past year, Zack made this point more eloquently than me. We, because we are mortal men, sometimes avoid reflection because we know we're not perfect. Some of what we are feels ugly because some of what we are *is* ugly. You must create space in your heart to accept the truth, forgive yourself, and slowly evolve into something different and good. Without this space, it will be very difficult to reflect on hard but exceedingly important questions.

The toughest questions you can ask yourself are: Why am I here? What matters to me? What is good? Am I good? Why was I put on this earth? These questions are not just part of the work: *they are the work*. These questions are ones you will want to avoid talking about, even with people you love, trust, and respect, because they are *big*—but you must. Do not shy away from these questions simply because they are hard. You may go your whole life without asking them and have decades of regret.

One day, your Dada and I had a conversation about what he liked, wanted, and cared about. I was asking him questions, sincerely and simply. I remember where we were standing in the kitchen, around the island at Dadi's house. It was in the evening and dark. Your Dada was in his early sixties. He seemed to have a powerful revelation and told me nobody had ever asked him questions like that before and he feared it was too late for him to change anything about his life, health, and habits. Part of me (though I know his death wasn't my fault) wonders if he would still be here if I, or anyone else, had asked him those questions earlier in his life. Would he have been more at peace? Less stressed? Would he have taken better care of his health if he had had a better connection with his soul, hopes, and dreams? I will never know. Despite my guilt, I am relieved I was able to talk about such things with my father and that he was able to open his heart, even if for a moment, to me, his son. This is one moment I have treasured most in my life, despite it being painful for my father to talk about those things. It was the moment we went from being father and child, to being two men. To being two *friends*. After that moment, we seemed to have an unspoken understanding of, and respect for, each other. I respected your Dada for the courageous way he persisted through a difficult life, and he respected me for finally appreciating how hard life can really be.

I hope, my sons, that you will open your heart—with and without my help—so we may someday reflect on questions of the heart together. It will be difficult, but I have no doubt in my mind and heart that you will find it well worth the challenge.

Love,
Papa

* * *

9

Truth

No lie is small.

August 21, 2017

Boys,

In these letters, I am suggesting a particular moral way of approaching how you live as part of a greater community: *Be a good person. Resist the corrupting influence of power. Act in a way that builds trust amongst people.* To be sure, doing this is layered, difficult, and fuzzy. In my observation, people seem to want answers, lists, and pithy catchphrases that help them shortcut thinking deeply about the ineluctable questions before them. Many internet articles have been clickbait of the "top ten ways to get promoted after just 6 months" ilk. Maybe I'm being unfair because it's certainly not everyone, and I only have about 30 years of anecdotal data backing up this claim, but it seems to me that the general tendency toward fast answers remains in America today. There are plenty of books, websites, and companies that offer a bullet-pointed version of anything about which you want a shallow, wrapped-into-a-bow sort of opinion.

I don't think anyone can offer you a top 10 list or infographic on how to be a good person in 5 simple steps. But let's say someone managed to distill goodness and the work into a set of bullet points. I don't think it would be helpful. To walk the path of goodness with consistency, you must learn certain lessons and internalize them deeply. It's not a matter of knowing them in your mind, those lessons must be embodied. It's not good enough to memorize axioms related to goodness and then say you get it. Walking the path of goodness is not an exercise in memory or intellect. You must make what you learn part of every single moment of your life and understand it deeply. There are no shortcuts; shallow platitudes don't work. There's no way to avoid the hard work.

I realized early on in writing these letters to you that I had no "answers" for what to do to become a good person. There is no explicit set of rules you can just follow. I can't give you the answers to the test, but I can give you advice on how to build the capacity to figure out the answers for yourself. I can't tell you a set of rules that will suddenly make you a good person, but just as an athletic trainer can advise you on exercises that build strength and muscle mass directly, I can teach you how to build the capacity for goodness within yourself. I can teach you how to do the work. In my reflections, I have come to believe there are three critical pillars of the work: (1) the work to build curiosity; (2) the work to build courage; and (3) the work to build persistence. I see the job of helping you to develop these three capacities to be among the highest duties I have as your father. Also, curiosity, courage, and persistence are capacities I work doggedly to develop in myself.

Where to start? We must start with the truth. Be honest. That is what your Dada and Dadi impressed most upon me, and it is the most important lesson I can impart to you three. Honesty means two things: being honest with yourself and being honest with others. Honesty is the root of living a good and virtuous life. If you can do that, you will likely figure out the rest of this puzzle of goodness by struggling through it yourself. Honesty is the foundation of goodness. Without honesty, curiosity, courage, and persistence cannot follow.

Be Honest with Others

No lie is small. At times, people will try to tell you otherwise in your life, and at times you'll try to convince yourself of the same. No matter the subject, no matter the stakes, no lie is a small lie. Some lies may have lesser consequences, but all lies are big, and they matter because they cause harm in various ways—every single one. As moral men, we are not omniscient. When we speak, we cannot always have absolute certainty in what we are saying. We must act with the faith that what we believe is true *actually is* true. I think the sandwich I am eating won't kill me, but I don't know that for sure. I think I made plans to meet a friend at a certain time, and that I can make it there on time, but I don't know that for sure. Even under the best circumstances, when we believe something to be true, we may be operating with uncertainty. Because we are not omniscient, we have no choice but to make decisions amidst uncertainty. And sometimes, because of that uncertainty, the consequences of our actions cause us (or others) suffering, even when it's not our intention. For example, I may believe with my whole heart that our vacation flight departs at 4:23p.m., but we miss our flight because it departed at 3:23p.m. You may tell me that the only items your mother asked me to purchase from the store are carrots and garbage bags, until we get home and realize we forgot that she needed chocolate chips for the cookies we're supposed to bake for family dinner. When we don't know or remember the truth with 100% omniscience, sometimes the consequences of our actions cause harm to ourselves or others, even if it's not our intent to do so. We're not perfect, these moments are part of life.

What makes lying horrible is that the liar is adding to the uncertainty *on purpose*. It's already a reality of human life that we make decisions amidst uncertainty with the risk of painful consequences. A lie *adds* to that uncertainty and risk, *deliberately*. The liar, therefore, is making it more likely that pain, suffering, or harm occurs during the normal course of life. It may be the case that the pain is minor, but the fact remains: to lie is to deliberately set someone up to make a bad decision or face some increased level of harm.

Even seemingly small lies can add up to much greater harm. Let's say your mother asked me to purchase a turnip as part of our weekly grocery run. I don't particularly like turnips, so let's say I lied and told her that the turnips were out so I could avoid having to eat the turnip. But what I didn't know was that your mother needed a turnip for some sort of recipe she was preparing with a friend at work for a potluck in the office. Your mother promised turnips, and I lied to cover up the fact that I didn't want to buy one. So now your mother must make an extra stop on her way home from work tomorrow to purchase a turnip, at a cost of 30 minutes wasted that she would otherwise have had. This may seem like a small inconvenience, but this annoyance of an extra run to the store easily compounds over time.

Let's say I were a habitually dishonest husband who told "little" lies once a week. Each time I lied, it would waste 30 minutes of your mom's time. Over the course of the rest of our lives, that would result in over 1000 hours wasted (.5 hours per week x 52 weeks x 40 years = 1040 hours). Conservatively, that 1040 hours would waste 43.3 days of your mother's life over the course of 40 years (1040 hours wasted / 24 hours in a day), and that becomes even more time—65 days—if you adjust for the fact that we generally only have 16 waking hours a day (1040 waking hours wasted / 16 hours awake per day). So that would be sixty-five whole days wasted because of the seemingly "little" lies I'm telling. Those 65 days are valuable. When you are young, 65 days might not seem like a long time— that's half a semester of algebra or about 9 weeks of soccer practice. *Sixty-five days of one's life is not a huge burden over the course of 40 years*, you might say. But oh, what a loss that would be.

As you age, you may begin to have the realizations I have started to have: time is by far the most precious thing we have, and we never get it back, not one minute. When you are young, you are rich in time, so wasting a little doesn't feel painful. As we age, however, we become poorer in time. I have less time on this Earth now than I did 10 minutes ago, and that pool of time is always shrinking and fading away as the clock advances. Sometimes I imagine what it would be like to be on my deathbed, hopefully in my eighties or nineties after a long, full life. Even after a long and full life, I know I would trade time if I could. If I was on my deathbed, ready to pass, what would I not trade for an extra day, or even an extra few hours with your mother? Or with you and the families you will have of your own by then. If I could trade all the money I had left for one extra hour with our family, when my soul was on the precipice of being released into the undiscovered country, I would. Don't you think you would too? Sixty-five days, leeched out in 30-minute increments weekly, may not be a grave loss to a young man but, to an old man, 65 extra days would be a temptation to bargain with the devil.

Seemingly "little" lies also have other grave consequences, including broken trust. If I lied to your mother, I would be giving her a very good reason not to trust me. Because I lied once, she'd have a strong (and reasonable) inclination that I will lie again. Why would (or should) she believe what I say if I lied to her once? If I lied once, there must be some deeper motivation or character flaw at play, and that which led to the lie is unlikely to be resolved quickly or on its own. But even if the lie I tell is "small" and, for whatever reason, she thought enough of me to keep our relationship, she'd still have doubt, most likely about whether I am telling the truth. The next time I go to the grocery store, she would be reasonable to think, "Did the store really not have dark chocolate, or is he lying again?" That might evolve into something like, "Is he really working late, or is he trying to get out of parental responsibilities?" And then later, "Did we really exceed our home renovation budget, or is he buying stuff without telling me?" And then at the very end of the line, "He says 'I love you,' but does he really mean it? Can I be safe with him?" It is often said that it takes a long time to build trust, but only one moment to lose it. Lies sow the seeds of doubt in a relationship between people and those doubts have far-reaching implications.

Doubt is what causes individuals to go through the arduous, time-consuming, and expensive process of drawing up legal contracts and squabbling over them because, if you doubt whether someone will keep his word, that's a valid reason for a contract to be written and penalties to be specified for non-compliance. Doubt causes certain sellers to collect a deposit anytime someone rents an apartment. Doubt is what causes us to believe (and waste time and energy) on ridiculous falsehoods and conspiracy theories that cast suspicion on scientific facts and delay the implementation of sound public policy. More generally, doubt in others is what pressures us into tipping the scales of decisions in favor of our short-term, self-oriented interests, rather than our long-term common interests. After all, why would I take a risk for the common good if I think my teammate or my neighbor is going to drop the ball, renege on the deal, or try to stiff me? I wouldn't want to be the sucker holding the bag, would you? Lies cause us to doubt our relationships with others, which is to say that lies are something that cause us to doubt communities themselves. Over time, lies destroy communities because doubt adds friction and tension to relationships, and over time, with enough of those frayed bonds, communities implode. A community, in essence, is a web of relationships united by a shared vision. Lies cause those relationships—which define and serve as the underlying foundation of a community—to dissolve, and eventually cause the community to fail.

The consequences of lying are substantial and not only harm those lied to, but also the community, by undermining the bonds of trust they depend on to exist.

Be Honest with Yourself

Lying to yourself is a bit of an abstract concept. We believe something we know or suspect isn't true. This happens more than you might think. The best example I can think of to illustrate how this happens comes from dating. From the time I had crushes on girls in middle school to the little dating I did before I met your mother, I let myself believe things about feelings—my own or a woman's—that I knew, deep down, weren't true. Maybe I thought someone would want to go on a date with me when there was no sign that they did. Or maybe I knew someone might like to go on a date with me, but I was too afraid to ask them, so I pretended that any indications of interest they had were just a coincidence. The easiest way out of those uncomfortable realities was to lie to myself.

I have also wanted something so much to be the truth, I tried to pretend it into existence. Or I gave myself the benefit of the doubt to the point of delusion so I could hold on to false hope. But as it happens, my sons, the truth is the truth whether we want it, believe it, or want to believe it. I've lied to myself more times than I am proud of. It happened when I tried to convince myself that travel wasn't destroying me when I worked as a consultant. It happened when Nakul—your Cha Cha—went ahead and I pretended like his death didn't affect me that much. It happened when I thought, *one more drink wouldn't matter*. It happened when someone I love did something hurtful and I wanted to let them off the hook, so I pretended it wasn't a big deal. It's happened when I've thought, *I'm not too busy, I can say yes to this.* There are many times in your life when what you want to be true is easier and more desirable and convenient than the actual truth; you will want to believe it, even just for

81

a moment, and you'll think it's okay. But it's crucial that you don't give in to those falsehoods because the same injuries that occur when you lie to others—harm, doubt, and distrust—occur when you lie to yourself. You will suffer from the same consequences of misinformation when making decisions. You will have doubt and distrust. For example, you might foolishly believe a stock price will rise, and buy a hundred shares, not because the facts suggest the price will rise, but because you *want* the facts to suggest that. If you make that trade of one hundred shares once, you might get lucky and not lose much money. But if you make that delusional trade of a hundred shares a hundred times, you might go broke. The harm of lying to yourself goes deeper than surface level. Lying to yourself makes it harder to trust your own judgment.

Truth and Curiosity

We don't discover goodness incidentally. We must seek to answer the most difficult question: *Am I good?* When you ask that question, will you tell the truth, or will you lie? Will you trust yourself or will you doubt the veracity of your answer? Will you tell yourself what you *wish* were true? Taking the long walk toward goodness requires constant inquiry, reflection, and tenacious curiosity; we must turn that curiosity toward ourselves and look inward. This, my sons, is when the stakes of telling the truth are highest.

There are so many times lying has been easier and yielded some material benefit, whether it was a couple of bucks saved on a warranty claim or the chance to avoid a difficult conversation. Often, believing what I want to believe hurts my heart less. It's so tempting to give in and lie, even when

I know—with full certainty—that it's wrong or that my lie may have devastating long-term impacts on the lives of others or my own life. *How Papa,* you might ask, *do you stand your ground and not give into the seduction and temptation of a lie?* The easy answer is to never start lying. The more you behave with honesty and truthfulness, the more it will become a habit. You will eventually be so comfortable with telling the truth and so abysmally bad at lying, you will never want to lie. The harder answer is to come clean. This means being honest after lying and reconciling with all the people you have wronged and hurt. It means feeling the pain that that lie caused in your belly. Coming clean also means the acceptance of who we are.

What we least want to accept is that we are mortal, imperfect men; what we most need to accept is what we want to believe the least. We are not all-powerful; *we must accept that.* We are not all-knowing or all-loving, *we must accept that.* We are fallible men, *and we must accept that.* Once we accept who we are, it's easier for us to be honest about everything else.

There are so many wonderful things that you are and that you will be, but you will not be perfect. Accepting this is hard because it means we are acknowledging that we will struggle, we will die, that we will hurt others and ourselves, that we will make mistakes. A beautiful thing can emerge from this acceptance: forgiveness. Once we accept who we are, and all our shortcomings, we can take the pressure off by forgiving ourselves for the imperfections and trauma borne from the reality of death with which we are born into this world. The Christian tradition focuses heavily on this. Jesus died for us, and from this love and sacrifice came the forgiveness of sins. This is what we have faith in. Forgiveness and faith are central ideas for the tradition in which you were baptized. I find this idea of love, forgiveness, and faith to be powerful, even as a non-baptized person. Once we accept who we are, then forgive ourselves for what we are not, we can move on. Christian or not; Hindu or not; Buddhist, Jewish, Muslim, atheist or not; the truth remains: for a chance to *truly* live, we must forgive, starting with ourselves. When we accept and forgive, we can then choose what to do. We can either try to be better, even though we will never be perfect, or we can stay as we are. The catch is, if we try to be better, we must accept that we will have to do extremely hard things.

Our choice is to be more good than we were yesterday, or we can give up on those hard things and give into our imperfections and sins without putting up a fight. This discussion may make you feel overwhelmed. You may be thinking: *How do I even have a chance to persevere through the struggle ahead?* My sons, when you doubt yourself and think about giving in, remember this: as sure as there is always darkness, there is always light. Even in the hardest of times, being a better man is never impossible. I will always support you with unconditional love and so will your mother; even in the scariest and darkest of times, *we love you.* When you are at the end of your rope, *we love you.* Even when we go ahead and move on to the galaxies and whatever is beyond, *we love you.* We love you, for who you are, and who you will be, no matter what. As sure as there is rain and sun, you can count on us to love you. And even if everyone else in the universe turns on you, even if you turn on yourself, and even if you believe God has somehow turned on you, *we love you*. Because of that, there is always hope. Even when mortality burdens you, with devastating effects, do not give up.

By making this choice, this wager on goodness, we are

choosing a path where we will face one hard thing after another; we are accepting we will have to do hard things to become better people, over and over. The act of doing what is right, even when it is hard, is a working definition of *courage*. We need tremendous courage to become better men.

Love,
Your Papa

* * *

10

Courage

Courage is an action.

December 9, 2017

My Sons,

Courage is choosing to do the right thing, even though we know it will be hard. Courage, therefore, is essential to walk the path of goodness. After all, what's more difficult than changing ourselves to be better? And we surely will need to be better.

If we're honest with ourselves, we will all find that we are not perfect - many of our choices will surely be motivated by power instead of goodness. Which means, if we want to walk the path of goodness we'll have to make different choices. We'll have to change to become better. Some changes will be easy, like my choice to put away my mobile phone at dinner. But easy changes like that are not ones I worry about much. To be sure, breaking small habits does take work (focus and repetition), but it's not *hard*. Some changes will be painfully hard and overwhelming. In my life, some of those hard changes include dealing with vices like alcohol or pornography, and tempering my addiction to the allure of career, prestige, and money.

When I first drafted this letter, Robert was already born, and every day has been a blessing. But even the wonderful, joyous occasion of his birth has not relieved me of the need to forgive. The fact that I can be angry about work, fatigue, politics, or anything, amidst so much joy, is humbling. I have many hard changes to make, and I need to be better so I can have a heart that's not impaired in its ability to love you, your mother, our God, our extended family, our friends, and our neighbors. Let me tell you, my sons, letting go of anger and being forgiving is damn hard. In a world that leans on the caricature of men as naturally angry creatures, it feels impossible to get out from under the suffocating weight of anger. But if walking the path of goodness is our supreme goal, we must have courage to do some of these difficult things.

Courage is mettle that must come from within. Some try to mimic it, but that does not last. Let us focus on how to cultivate and build courage on purpose. There are many examples of courage that have been published by skilled and interesting writers, such as *Profiles in Courage* by President John F. Kennedy. It's one of the only books I have ever read twice. (It's on our bookshelf at home; I suggest you read it sometime.) Many books on courage do not serve us here. They give examples of men and women who have acted with courage, and that is instructive, but to get a sense of the *how* of courage, we need to peer into the mind and history of those individuals. We need to understand their inner voice and spirit and how they were developed. Examples of courage in those books often describe the last leg of the journey, rather than the journey itself. Comparing it to a theatrical play, the most common books on courage are a plot summary and a critic's review of the show's final performance, rather than a meticulous study of the auditions, rehearsals, and stagecraft that happened for hundreds of hours before the curtain rose. Comparing it to an athletic team, those books are a recap of the game, rather than a meticulous study of the practices, team meetings, and weight room workouts that prepared the team to play at their highest potential.

The most elegant way I can think of to describe how courage works is to compare it to an airplane. Let me first describe to you, in layman's terms, how an airplane flies. To fly, an airplane must overcome the force of gravity placed upon it by the gravitational pull of the Earth. The force of gravity is the hard stuff we need to do to become better men. For an airplane, the design of the wing is what overcomes this force. The design is simple. It is basically a board that is flat on the bottom and curved on top. When air moves over the wing, lift occurs: the force that pushes against gravity to allow the plane to fly. The curved shape causes air to have higher pressure on the bottom of the wing than at the top and deflects air downward, causing lift. Courage is what we need to do hard things, just as lift is what an airplane needs to overcome the force of gravity and fly. To get enough air to flow over the wing and generate lift, the plane must move—fast. The force that pushes the plane forward is called thrust. Thrust is generated by the airplane's engines. Once the thrust of the engines pushes the plane forward, it causes air to move over the wing, which leads to lift being generated. But, in addition to gravity, lift, and thrust, there is one more force needed for airplanes to fly: we must account for drag. Drag slows the plane down. The force of thrust generated by the engines must overcome the drag put onto the airplane as it moves forward. This is an oversimplified explanation of the physics behind flight, please forgive me for that. Maybe someday you will be a more accomplished physicist or engineer and you can explain lift to me in a more sophisticated way.

But if you'll indulge me for just another moment, let me summarize what this analogy tells us about courage. First, for lift to be generated, air must flow over the wing, which means the plane must move. For the plane to move, the thrust of the engines must be greater than the force of the drag. This is the same with courage. Courage is an action. It is not something that happens when we are standing still. Just like a plane, in our lives, we will experience drag—realities that pull us back and deter us from acting, from moving forward. But just like a plane, we can generate thrust, we can generate forces that push us forward and into motion. Just like for a plane, however, to generate sufficient forward motion, the thrust we create must be stronger than the drag pulling us backward. So, we will examine how to reduce the drags that pull us backward and how to increase the thrusts that push us forward. Thrust must be greater than drag.

To generate lift, especially when carrying a heavy load, it's not enough to have a bit more thrust than drag. Having thrust exceed drag only ensures the plane will move forward, not that it will fly. For a plane to fly, the air flowing over the wing must be going fast enough to generate enough lift to overcome the force of gravity. This is why planes don't start to lift off the ground and fly until they pick up a certain amount of speed. The same goes for us: the more difficult the challenge ahead, the more courage we need to lift us off the ground and fly. But to fly, we cannot only have a *little* more thrust than drag, we need *a lot* more thrust than drag. The harder the challenge, the greater the difference needs to be between thrust and drag.

There's an interesting paradox here that your mom and I were talking about on the way back from our monthly brunch club. (It was the day I wrote this letter. Robert was only six weeks old, so it would be silly to expect him to remember this conversation, although we all know his memory is unmatched.) Your mom is a wise woman. This point would have been lost on me for months if not for talking to her. The paradox is that the choices and habits that affect the forces of drag and thrust in our lives the most are usually not the biggest, seemingly most consequential life decisions, but the small ones we make every day, often without paying them much thought. Courage is most affected by the small decisions we make over and over from muscle memory. Here's a quick example of what I mean: There are some nasty emotions that affect your ability to do things that are hard, like stress, fear, and anger. These emotions zap the mental energy out of you, leaving little to spare for courageous action. These are three of the biggest forces of drag I can think of. You must manage and neutralize them; they cannot be ignored for long. To keep moving forward, we must deal with stress, fear, and anger in a healthy, effective way. I personally have to write (surprise, surprise) or talk with someone. Maybe what's effective for you is exercise or analytical meditation. Different strategies work for different people. Something small that will happen almost every day (and certainly every day you speak with your mom or me) is someone asking you a very simple question: "How are you doing today?" When someone asks you that question, you must make a choice that will likely be from muscle memory. As you answer the question, you will choose the words you will use. You will have to decide whether you will acknowledge how you are feeling or whether you will just say, "I'm doing fine," without thinking about it. You will have to decide whether to look inward and discern whether you are feeling scared, sad, joyous, or peaceful, or whether you will ignore the emotion going on inside of you.

Even if you are only asked "How are you?" once a day, after a year you will have made the decision of whether or not to probe your emotional state three hundred and sixty-five times. If you were stressed, fearful, or angry, you will have had three hundred and sixty-five opportunities to ignore your emotions and let your fear, anger, and stress build. Every one of those muscle memory choices to ignore your emotions may not be that consequential on their own, but in aggregate, the consequences are enormous.

In my first letter to you, I told you about the time I was most stressed, fearful, and angry. It's probably not surprising to hear that it was also the time I chose not to acknowledge those very difficult emotions. There was a point where I couldn't complete the sentence "I feel…" when speaking to someone. No wonder I was having such a hard time putting my wager on goodness instead of power.

Certainly, the big moments and big decisions in life matter. These are the moments your mom and Granddad call inflection points. How we act in these inflection points—like choosing who to marry, how to react to death, or how to choose a vocational path—are a big deal. These inflection points, and others, define us and can have long-lasting effects on our life. But these inflection points don't truly help us cultivate courage. They don't shape and mold us into courageous people because they just don't happen often enough to add up. What your mother was suggesting, and I agree, is that seemingly little decisions—like how we respond to someone asking how we are doing—are the moments that shape whether or not we reduce drag and increase thrust in our lives. Little everyday moments are the training ground for cultivating courage within us so we can meet the moment at inflection points when the stakes are highest. Just as in tennis, you won't be able to just go onto the court and hit a dynamite backhand on a high-stakes match point. You would have hit that backhand thousands of times in practice when the stakes were low.

So, my sons, don't get caught up in the grand, dramatic inflection points and think those are the moments you become courageous. Those moments matter, but they, paradoxically, aren't the ones that matter most when trying to develop courage. The small decisions you make over and over, every day, are the moments you can practice and develop the capacity for courage.

The questions you might be asking now are: *What "forces" influence courageous action, and how do I practice and shape them in my day-to-day life? How do I "reduce the drags" and "increase the thrusts"?* Those, my sons, are precisely the right questions, and exactly what we will explore in detail now. Let's begin.

Love,
Your Papa

* * *

II

2018

11

Fear and Anger

Love is our thrust.

April 16, 2018

My Sons,

Shane Parrish, founder of the Farnam Street blog, turned me on to an important idea that echoes through many aspects of my life. It applies to courage. It's the difference in how one behaves depending on if one is an amateur or a professional. The idea is simple. Amateurs and professionals need to approach the game they are playing differently. Professionals can and should attempt high-risk moves. In other words, professionals should play to win. On the other hand, amateurs, who have less skill and experience and are prone to making mistakes, should take the opposite approach: they should play not to beat themselves.

The logic is straightforward. If you are masterful at something, take the hard shots because you have done the work that prevents you from beating yourself. If you're not an expert, focus on the basics and forget the fancy stuff, otherwise you *will* beat yourself.

Here's an example from tennis, a sport your mother and I love and grew up playing. In tennis, you will often spar back and forth with an opponent. Some shots, like a drop shot or a spin-laden serve, take more finesse than others. Most people I have played tennis with (including myself) love to hit finesse shots—even though they are hard to execute—because those shots look cool, feel cool, and end points quickly. The problem with this strategy is the net. If you don't hit a shot perfectly, it's easy to hit it straight into the net, which means the point ends and you've lost it. In tennis parlance, this is called an unforced error because you made a mistake and ended the point—your opponent didn't have to do anything other than let you screw up. The fact that you hit the ball into the net during a rally is "unforced" by your opponent, it's all on your racket.

You can guess the lesson here. When you're an amateur, attempting a low-percentage finesse shot often results in an unforced error at the bottom of the net. Over the course of a match, you end up losing without your opponent having to do much: you beat yourself. The alternative strategy is to just get the ball back over the net. Nothing fancy, just dink it across and let the other guy mess up. For professionals, it's prudent to hit higher-risk shots because they are able to execute them and use a mix of shots to put themselves in an offensive stance and win points outright. Professionals can hit "winners" deliberately. To hit winners, amateurs need a lot of luck.

The same dynamic exists with courage. Before you try to adopt complex ideas and behaviors, focus on not beating yourself. Succumbing to fear and anger are equivalent to beating yourself in a tennis match by hitting the ball into the net. Where I started, and what I suggest, is to neutralize the fear and anger in your heart before you try to do the difficult and complex finesse shots it takes to build courage. I chose to highlight fear and anger rather than emotions like sadness and jealousy because those mind states have held me back from personal transformation and sacrifice in my life. More than that, fear and anger are debilitating because of the reactions they elicit. Other difficult emotions feel like a cannonball chained to your leg while swimming, making everything else harder. For me, fear and anger were particularly debilitating because they caused me to avoid swimming altogether. They are not only drags—they are *paralyzing*.

What Are Fear and Anger?

Fear and anger are caused by dissonance. The object of dissonance is different, however, for fear and for anger. Anger is a dissonance of expectations about the past. I expected, wanted, or thought I deserved one thing, but what happened was another. I expected to be treated well by the waiter, but I wasn't—that made me angry. I wanted to have pie for dessert, but someone else ate the last piece—that made me angry. I wanted to have a peaceful afternoon with my family, but our local park was bombed by a warring nation—that made me angry. When it comes to doing hard things, anger is a potent distraction. When I am angry, it's all I can think about. I spend lots of time and energy being angry. That's time and energy stolen from doing the important work of goodness.

I don't like to feel angry, so when I am, a few things happen.

First, I might try to numb or displace it. That would be okay if anger could be numbed or displaced easily or safely. As it turns out, that's not the case. Anger cannot be put in a bag and hustled into a trash canister, never to be seen again. It strikes back. What's worse, anger can make a person do crazy things that are hurtful, stupid, or both, to others and themselves. We think we can neutralize anger through things like alcohol, but those approaches only work for a little while, and in the time our anger is postponed, it usually gets worse. Which is to say: if you're going to deal with anger—and I mean real, bona fide anger—in any effective way, it's going to take everything you've got. If you're dealing with anger, you're not going to have anything left for personal transformation or sacrifice for others. Anger is like a wildfire; it consumes everything in sight until not a single tree or flower is left. Fear, on the other hand, is not caused by a dissonance of expectations about the past, but by a dissonance of uncertainty about the future. I think I'll be able to keep my job, but a recession is coming, so I experience fear. Michigan is up two points in a Final Four matchup, but there's a lot of clock left—that induces fear. I know I will die, but I'm not sure when—that creates fear. Fear, as I have lived it, is what you get when you have doubts about whether what you want to happen will happen. Much like anger, when it comes to doing hard things, fear is a distraction. More potently, fear causes avoidance. It causes us to avoid attempting hard things, like personal transformation and sacrifice, because they are not certain. Fear biases us to favor the status quo, even if we do not like the way things currently are.

Let's take an easy-to-describe fear, like flying on an airplane, as an example. I love airplanes, as you'll come to know, but let's say I fear them. Imagine I am contemplating taking a new job; not just any job, a really good job, one much better than the one I have. And not just a job that pays well and is with a respected company, but one that is meaningful and helps people. Say it's my dream job. But there's a catch. I will have to travel on planes for this job. This is a problem because I'm terribly afraid of flying. This leaves me with a choice: either confront my fear or turn down the job offer. Fear creates avoidance and helps to preserve the status quo.

Not all instances of fear and avoidance are benign. What if your fear is of retaliation for reporting your boss for sexually harassing one of your colleagues? What if your fear is the shame of admitting an addiction? What if your fear is of the argument that might ensue if you try to work out a problem you have with your spouse? Sometimes letting your fears stop you from doing the right thing can have very real and undesirable consequences.

As we have seen with these examples, fear and anger distract you from, and cause you to avoid, choosing goodness and choosing the work. Luckily, you don't have to submit to fear and anger. There are things, within your locus of control, that you can do to neutralize the fear and anger you have. Let's turn to some of these strategies now.

Neutralizing Fear and Anger

The idea we just established was, on the surface, a simple one: fear and anger are reactions to expectations, which shows that expectations must exist for us to have fear and anger. After all, if we have no expectations about the past, what would we be angry about? If we have no expectations about the future, what could we fear? A seemingly simple remedy to fear and anger is to abandon expectations altogether.

I spoke about this idea with your mother some weeks ago. I was suggesting that forming expectations might not be prudent and that I should live with fewer of them. This suggestion is one that your mother rightly pushed back on. After all, there can be good reasons to have expectations, and times where it's not just nice, but important to have them. After thinking about it for a few weeks, I've come to agree with your mother. Expectations are important because it's difficult to have even the most basic intention without expectations of yourself and of others. Moreover, our form of government—constitutional democracy—has a deep concept of rights and liberties within it. We have *rights*. We can make expectations of the government on a reasonable number of things. We should expect freedom of speech, religion, and the press. We should expect the ability to cast a vote in elections. We should expect equal protection under the law. We should expect to be treated without discrimination on our sex, religion, sexual orientation, and race. Abandoning all expectations would remove reasonable boundaries we have to ensure our sovereignty and self-determination as humans. To have rights, we *must* have expectations. If we couldn't form expectations about the world or opted out of forming expectations, it would be difficult to contemplate anything outside our immediate survival. All we would think about is the moment we are in. What if we couldn't expect to sleep with a roof over our heads? Or that the floor under our feet would remain intact? What if we couldn't walk around our neighborhood and expect not to be assaulted, robbed, or shot? What if we couldn't expect that the lessons of how to be a better man yesterday would carry over to today? What if I couldn't expect you or your mother to love me? If we could not form expectations, we would be living in a state of chaos and intensity.

I learned about this firsthand while working on a team that was trying to prevent gang violence in Detroit. Some of the young men in our city, our neighbors, have had to contend with such a reality because their immediate safety and security is so directly and consistently threatened, they can't think more than a few hours into the past or future. The future, for these young men, is *that* uncertain. They have been living in a state of flux their whole lives. It breaks my heart that these neighbors of ours are living in a constant state of siege because of any number of things like poverty, food security, violence, or trauma.

In a way, we left the state of nature and formed communities so we could form expectations about the world more concretely and have the capacity to think about things beyond survival. Now, reflecting on what your mother said, it's preposterous to try to remove expectations—that would be a volatile way to live. We need to form expectations to be able to live useful lives. If we can't abandon all expectations, perhaps what we can do is not take what we expect for granted. I expect to have a roof over my head, but it may not happen. If it does, I am grateful, but I realize there are no guarantees. The Bhagavad Gita contains timeless wisdom around the idea of expectations. In chapter 2, verse 47, Lord Krishna says to Arjuna:

> *You have a right to perform your prescribed duties, but you are not entitled to the fruits of your actions. Never consider yourself to be the cause of the results of your*

activities, nor be attached to inaction.

Lord Krishna is suggesting that we must continue to act and do our duty; we need to conduct our lives by being people of action who do not worry about the past or the future. What we need to abandon is not our expectations (because doing our duty requires expectations), but our attachment to *the fruits* that result.

Non-attachment is an ideal state that takes consistent practice over a lifetime, such as through yoga and its eight-limb path, or through Buddhist practice. But non-attachment is not the only helpful concept for dealing with fear and anger. Let's explore two others: (1) developing more accurate and tolerant expectations so they are consistent with reality; and (2) learning to react better when our expectations are not met.

More Accurate and Tolerant Expectations

Earlier, we discussed the importance of being honest with ourselves. What's unfortunate is that our brain makes it easy to fool ourselves. The term for this is *cognitive bias*. Cognitive biases cause us to think in flawed ways; for example, giving disproportionally more credit to ourselves when things go well and assigning disproportionate blame to others when things go badly.

There are many other cognitive biases that are well documented, which I won't go into here, but a good way to combat them is to learn about what they are and use a process to think through decisions that account for, and help curb, the effects of these biases. One cognitive bias that's relevant to our discussion of expectations is the *optimism bias*. Optimism bias is basically this: we believe situations will turn out better than they probably will. This is obviously a bad bias to have when trying to set accurate and tolerant expectations because these expectations will be skewed toward a reality that is rosier than what life really is. Luckily, I have found that there is one relatively straightforward way to temper an optimism bias: we must be students of history. We must gather data (through experience; listening to others; reading; etc.) of comparable situations and accept them. Once this is done, we must also accept that what happens to us is unlikely to deviate greatly from the mean of others' long-run experiences. When I suggest being a student of history, I don't mean grasping 1-2 recent examples of comparable events, I mean exploring the widest possible sample you could reasonably consider in the time you have available to learn. When you are considering history, it is unhelpful to cherry-pick only what you want to see. To have accurate expectations, we must gather sufficient, representative data related to our current situation, and we must think about that data probabilistically.

Another advantage of studying history is that it helps us understand the range of others' experiences and the spectrum of possible outcomes that may occur: we can make the range of possibilities we expect ever wider. We can be more tolerant of extreme outcomes if they are already in our mind's range of possible outcomes.

While I am suggesting that a range of outcomes can be observed over a long-run history, I am not saying your life is beholden to that history. Every situation is different, and every person is different, it's just that in the long run, systems tend to regress toward the mean. Again, I am not saying your life is relegated to whatever the long-run mean is, but

103

that if you want outcomes that deviate from the mean, your actions must deviate from history. I am also not suggesting that when you adopt accurate and tolerant expectations, you give up hope for what's possible. Hope and expectations are different modes of the mind. You can have high hopes without having inaccurate and intolerant expectations. Expectations are about the *probability* of our wants being satisfied. Hope is about the *possibility* of our wants being satisfied.

Ideally, if we were able to have more accurate and tolerant expectations, we wouldn't have to deal with as much fear or anger because the dissonance between our expectations and reality would be lessened. As we know, anything can happen in life. Life can be so unpredictable, it's unreasonable to think our expectations will always be accurate and tolerant of variation. So, let's consider how we might shape how we react when our expectations are inaccurate or intolerant, so when life happens, we wouldn't, as easily, escalate to a state of anger or fear.

Shaping Our Reactions to Inaccurate and Intolerant Expectations

You may hear people say they cannot change. Or that they are too old to change. I believe this is false. Everyone's experiences, knowledge, and behaviors change who they are every single day. There is a proverb, said by Heraclitus, a pre-Socratic philosopher, that captures this idea well:

> *No man ever steps in the same river twice, for it's not the same river and he's not the same man.*

We change every day. The world around us changes every day. It's not that everyone can change, it's that everyone *already does* change. That's not up for debate. To suggest otherwise simply isn't correct.

What people really mean when they say, "I can't change" is that they are either not willing to change in an intentional way, or they do not know how to change in an intentional way. You or others might not believe you can change how you react when facing inaccurate and intolerant expectations, but *you can.* It's not easy, but as we've discussed, it's crucially important and worth the effort.

Shaping how you react is not a one-time investment. It is a practice you must engage in constantly. I do not have an exhaustive list of behaviors that will help you create this practice. Nobody does. But I will share the best ideas I have in hopes they will be helpful as you create your practice to intentionally shape how you react to inaccurate and intolerant expectations.

1. Over time, developing a **reflection practice** has been the most potent way to shape my intentions and actions.

2. Another general principle is to **operate from a position of strength**. If you are vulnerable, and in a position where one mistake will send your whole life into a tailspin, you will have pressure on your shoulders that will make you reactive. But there are lots of ways to operate from a position of strength. Live within your means, build up a rainy day fund, and don't pile on debt. Build redundancy and over invest in things that are truly important, like life insurance, friendships, family, canned food, unallocated time, sleep, exercise, and more.

3. Build a **spiritual practice**, whether religious, spiritual, or contemplative. There are many paths to help you stay centered.

4. **Meditate**. Meditation has proven to help with stress and anxiety, in addition to having other mind-body benefits.

5. Monitor your **information diet**. Information is like food. It can nourish you, but if it's junk, it will make you obese and ill. Make sure you are exposing yourself to a wide variety of nutritious information, diverse sources, and perspectives.

—

We could talk at great length about these, and we will, either in subsequent letters I write to you, or as you grow up. You can count on that. But before I close this subject about fear and anger, let's turn to one more topic: how we deal with them.

If you are anything like me, you wouldn't like admitting—to yourself or others—that you're feeling fear or anger. I don't like feeling those emotions, and I doubt you will. They're not comfortable, nor should they be—we don't behave our best when subdued by fear or activated by anger, and so it would be a natural reaction to hide, ignore, or deny them. For too long in my life, I hid, ignored, and rejected what I was feeling. As aforementioned, there were times, in my mid-twenties, when I said the phrase "I feel..." out loud and I couldn't finish the sentence. I was so out of touch with my emotional state, I was incapable of saying one word to describe how I felt out loud.

I hope to help you practice acknowledging your feelings. To be disconnected from the expression of your soul is a dark reality indeed. But you cannot depend on me forever. It is essential that you look inward and listen to how you are feeling. To do that is to be human.

There are many ways to reveal the feelings shrouded within. I like to write, dance, and talk with close friends. You might sing, paint, or write poetry. Maybe you would like to talk to a counselor or pastor. You can also read about emotions to develop greater emotional granularity—just having the language to specifically express emotions makes a difference. *Atlas of the Heart* by Brené Brown is on our bookshelf at home; it has helped me to develop fluency in the language of emotions.

Whatever you must do to access and contemplate your feelings, do it. If you don't, you will likely take a destructive route: alcohol; drugs; or worse. I will try my hardest to not fail you on this and will listen carefully and patiently to you so you will feel safe sharing your feelings with me.

Once you have acknowledged having fear or anger, you must find ways to understand, express, and explore your emotions without hurting yourself or others. This is not easy. More than anything, I talk about my feelings, usually with your mother. I also write. Of course, exercise, dance, and meditation are helpful, and as I have gotten older, prayer and the loving presence of God have become refuges for me.

There is a type of fear and anger precipitated by moments in which we are treated cruelly by others. When you are mistreated in your life—and it will happen—it will probably cause you to feel fear or anger, and maybe even hopelessness or despair. In those moments, your involuntary reflex may be to reciprocate those feelings by treating someone else cruelly. When being mistreated, I have found it hard to release my fear and anger; rather, I lust for vengeance. Even today, I came home from work and felt as if there was a degree of cruelty inflicted upon me by what felt like the whole world. We had dealt with an ice storm and gone to stay with Mimi and Granddad. I had had a meeting at work where I had been afraid of being shamed in front of my colleagues. Beyond this, the real reason for feeling this way is that today would have been your Dada's 67th birthday and I miss him. I grieve him still. I grieve the birthday parties you will never have with him, and the cake you will never share with him. I know so clearly how much he would have loved you and cherished every minute he would have spent with you. I know, with my full heart, how much he loves you all and watches over you three now. I grieve the memories you will never have of him on this Earth.

I have felt the linger of cruelty so much lately. The easiest thing for me to have done would have been to be lazy, angry, tense, and nasty to you, your mother, and your brothers. But I have not yet mentioned the greatest purifier of the heart. That purifier, my sons, is love. If you can find a way to show love to someone and develop a genuine concern for their well being, that love not only washes over them and heals them, but also you. The greatest neutralizer and elixir of fear and anger is love.

Today, when I came home, I saw you and your mother and it changed me. We played our usual games like jumping bean and tickle monster and, I swear to God, all the ugliness I was feeling and all the pain I was carrying evaporated from my limbs and soul. The opportunity to show my love to you, your mother, your brothers, and Riley is the greatest gift of my life. It is the tide that washes over me and brings me back to Oneness every day.

Hopefully, this letter has made it clear that keeping anger and fear out of your heart is essential because they make it difficult to do the hard stuff. If you can take courageous action on the hard work of bettering yourself, you will not be stuck and unable to progress down the path of goodness. But neutralizing fear and anger, and stopping there, doesn't guarantee courage. Once you have neutralized them, you must still choose to act on the really hard stuff the path of goodness compels. You must do the difficult, diligent preparation it compels. You must dig into the determination to start something and channel the persistence to keep going even when you stumble—and stumble you will. To actually *do* the work of goodness, dissolving fear and anger from your heart isn't enough in the same way minimizing drag on an airplane doesn't cause it to fly. We, just like the plane, also need to generate thrust. Even after removing those dragging influences of fear and anger, we need to be thrust from our state of rest and into a state of action and right conduct. The only force I know that is strong enough to do that is love. Love is our thrust.

But how to love? How to find it? How to open your heart to receive it? Let us search and stick to this essential question of courage to guide us: *how do we bring ourselves to do the very hard stuff that choosing goodness compels?* I suspect that if we stay true to that question, we will discern how to love and discover the source of its headwaters. Let us at least try.

Love,
Your Papa

* * *

12

Strong Ties, Humility, and Listening

The better we listen, the more its gravity draws us closer to love.

May 13, 2018

My Sons,

In my previous letter, we considered fear and anger because they are unforced errors you can intentionally avoid. By neutralizing them, you get out of your own way as you build courage to do the hard stuff. Choosing what to write about next was easy. I thought, *what is the most influential factor I can think of that affects behavior and choices, especially when it comes to the hard stuff?* The answer was simple: other people.

Let's discuss this notion of "other people" using a foundational concept from social network theory. In social network theory, a scholar named Mark Granovetter distinguished relationships as being in two categories: strong ties and weak ties. Strong ties are the people you have close, frequent contact with (like close friends and family). Weak ties are the relationships you have that are more distant and infrequent. Granovetter ended up doing some of the most influential work in sociology by showing that weak ties matter—a lot. Those weak ties can give you a critical piece of information to help you with a tough problem, whether it's how to change a car battery or a lead on a new job. Weak ties matter because information diffuses through them.

A newer scholar in the field of complexity and social networks, Damon Centola, wrote one of the most interesting books I've read in my adult life: *How Behavior Spreads: The Science of Complex Contagions.* Centola's work takes a slightly different tack. What his work demonstrates is that weak ties are great if you are trying to diffuse information and ideas throughout a network. But, if you want to change people's behavior, it happens through their immediate neighborhood of strong ties. I am extending his ideas a bit here, but the conclusion for us is straightforward: whether you have the courage to do hard things will be affected most by who your strong ties are, the people you are closest to, not your weak ties. Who you choose to surround yourself with and let grow into a strong tie is one of your most important life decisions, so choose wisely. Your choice will shape your strongest intentions and your most critical acts of courage. Weak ties help you to obtain novel information; strong ties influence whether you do the hard stuff.

Your Uncle B understands this through and through. He and I were talking shortly after he graduated high school, late at night, in the backyard of our family's place on Burt Lake. I was asking him about his transition from high school to college. Whatever we were talking about led him to share a pearl of wisdom I won't forget: "You are the product of the

111

top 5 people you spend the most time with," meaning, your most consequential intentions and choices—the choices about the hard stuff—are not fully determined by you. Your life, in turn, *is not fully determined by you*. Other people will have an influence on the most consequential moments of your life and the little moments that shape them. If you choose to live in a community, rather than the state of nature, you cannot avoid that influence. Your strong ties will nudge you, often strongly, toward choosing goodness or power. It's a done deal. What you do have some control over is who your strong ties will be. That's a choice—if you make it intentionally. Your Uncle B understands this clearly, which is why he's able to express this essential idea of the top 5 so elegantly.

So, why and how are strong ties so influential over the choices we make, particularly about the hard stuff? The following are the best reasons I can think of. First, it's feedback. One of the effects of our choice to come out of the state of nature is that we live in a community with other people with whom we interact. More specifically, as we make choices, the people around us react to them. They encourage what they like and discourage what they don't. The feedback we receive from others shapes our future choices and actions. The feedback we take most seriously (and receive most often) comes from our strong ties. Let me give you an example. One particularly difficult choice I have had to make lately was whether I would return to my job at Deloitte after graduate school. The stakes of that choice were high. Financially, I was choosing whether to walk away from my tuition being paid for, around $200,000, and a coveted spot at a top firm in the eyes of my peers. If I returned and stayed for two years, my tuition would be paid for. It wouldn't just be a financial impact; I would be walking away from perks and prestige too.

I mentioned what I was considering to my top 5. I was lucky to have really, *really* good people around me (and so are you). Nobody told me exactly what to do, but they did give me their honest take on the situation. They encouraged me to walk away from a job they saw was destroying my relationships and, in turn, my life. My top 5 nudged me to turn down the money and leave a prestigious consultancy. Many of my weak ties were surprised I was even considering the prospect of walking away from so much. As they politely questioned me about it, the culture around me, professionally, was to take the money and keep my placement at Deloitte. It was so much money and so practical as a setup for the rest of my career and, after all, only a two-year commitment. My weak ties nudged me toward taking the job, which is unsurprising in retrospect—not only was it rational from a financial and career perspective, but I probably would have been considered a more valuable connection to them if I worked for a prestigious firm.

My top 5 nudged me in a way that bucked the prevailing culture my weak ties were influencing me with. My closest people cared deeply about my well being and nudged me to not take that job and I didn't. Right or wrong, I was more strongly influenced by my top 5 than what the culture was telling me to do. Beyond that, my strong ties helped me to stay committed to the decision. I made a hard choice and their feedback and influence helped me to stick with it, even after I started waffling and questioning my decision.

The feedback we receive from our strong ties disproportionately affects the choices we make. Once we make a choice, their continued influence helps us stay committed. This is most true with who you choose to marry. Your mother is my strongest tie. Her influence, right or wrong, affects me the most. Thankfully, her influence on me—my choices, my character, my disposition—is the most benevolent in my life. She is an uncommonly good, loving, and thoughtful person. We are all lucky to have her in our top 5.

Our strong ties are one of the few things that can make or break us and influence the outcomes of our lives. They are one of the most consequential influences over whether we choose the work, walk the path of goodness, or succumb to the lust and trappings of power.

So, my sons, choose your top 5 wisely; if you have chosen them poorly, let them go. The pertinent "how" question is rather straightforward: How do you make good friends? I have found that you cannot just pick good friends; they cannot be bought, bullied, or flattered into spending time with you. Friends pick you. And people tend to choose those who like them. Truly good friends, the sort of ties that are strong and benevolent influences on your life and character, only come when YOU are a benevolent influence on their life and character. So focus on being a good friend who acts with good character, and you'll find yourself among good friends. The people who can't reciprocate your benevolent influence won't stick around.

What does being a good friend mean? A good friend shows up and is present in your life. A good friend tries to help you. A good friend tells you the truth, even when it's uncomfortable. A good friend treats you with love and respect. A good friend sets healthy boundaries and calmly tells you when those boundaries are being violated. A good friend acts like themselves around you. A good friend listens and shares. A good friend keeps good company. A good friend values his or her friends for who they are and not because of the money or status their friends may or may not have. A good friend isn't just good to their friends, but to everyone.

You can't mimic your way into being a good friend or person. Mimicry is fickle when the situation in front of you is hard. Being a good friend (and person) is not just a set of rules to follow, it's a mindset characterized by treating others with respect and putting the needs of others equal to or ahead of your own. The mindset of a good friend is perhaps characterized by compassion, a topic the Dalai Lama and Archbishop Desmond Tutu discuss prominently in *The Book of Joy: Lasting Happiness in a Changing World,* which they wrote in collaboration with Douglas Abrams. The mindset we need, they offer, is to have a genuine care and concern for other human beings. You must transform yourself into a good friend. That takes courage. When it comes to your top 5, the stakes are high, and the consequences are real.

When I originally wrote this letter, you, Bo, were about 6 months old. It is humbling and difficult for me to say this because, even at 6 months, I can't fathom how much I loved you. I can't fathom how quickly my love for you, Myles and Emmett, became unconditional as well. It is far more than simply to the moon and back, it is incalculable how much I love you all. I want to be attached to you, beyond the moon, the stars, and infinite galaxies.

What I have said, about letting negative influences go, is so important that it also applies to me. I pray deeply that I would never be anything but a benevolent influence in your life. But if I am steering you away from the path of goodness, you must stop letting me influence you. Even though it may break me if that were to happen. If I become a corrupting influence on

115

your life, you must box me out. Your lives, your character, and your souls are much more important than my happiness. I suppose that is why I'm so intent on finishing this book of letters about goodness. I so desperately want to understand how to be a better man and father so I can help you to become better. I want to earn my place in your lives. Perhaps by being a good man, I can justify being part of your lives and continue to be in a relationship of unconditional love with you all. To be part of a bond like that is something beautiful.

We have covered some ground on being courageous enough to transform yourself. Managing, avoiding, or coming to some sort of balance with fear and anger is one important cornerstone. Being intentional about your top 5 is another. These strategies alone, however, do not create courage, they merely remove some obstacles to achieving it. The bigger part of what leads to courage comes down to one last concept: humility.

Let's take all those behaviors of a good friend as an example—from listening and being yourself, to opening your heart. My lived experience has led me to conclude that we do the hard work of changing ourselves when we feel compelled to make sacrifices for others. We sacrifice for others if we value their needs at least as much as we value our own. People who think they are superior do not value others' needs equivalently to their own, people with humility do. Humility, in real life, is best represented by an attitude—that we are the same, and one is not better or more valuable than another—that makes it possible to consider the needs of others equivalently or more than our own.

I don't think the kind of humility that leads to sacrifice is something that falls from the sky or is fixed from birth. I believe it is a capability that can be developed and strengthened. Strengthening that muscle causes courage to emerge.

Now that we have plowed through some of the basics—fear, anger, and the importance of strong ties—let's dig into developing humility that leads to sacrifice.

Listening

I was going to take a break from writing and start transcribing my notes into a computer, which I hope you will find someday, tucked away, discreetly, in our family's office. I imagine you bored on a Sunday afternoon, stumbling upon the unlabeled notebooks, as sunlight pours through the windows and across the office walls. Maybe you'll plop down in the blue chair and start thumbing through the Moleskine's pages, trying to decipher my near-illegible handwriting—messages from an earlier, quieter time in our family history.

If you find the handwritten manuscript of these letters, you may notice the evolution to its final draft. The many handwritten pages I crossed out, excluded, or improved symbolize the tedious work of writing—yes—but more so, the evolution of thinking I have had on the subjects we have covered. These ideas were unfinished when I started, and they will be unfinished after I publish this volume. It will be up to us to refine them. Eventually, after I have gone ahead, they are for you to continue toiling on, so you may pass an unfinished draft of your own perspectives on to the families you are hopefully blessed to start someday.

We just celebrated your mother's first Mother's Day, which she loved every minute of. It was her first one with you here, Bo, and you made it a special one for her. Because of that special day, and time with you both, my spirit is renewed. I will hold off on transcribing notes for now. Let's keep talking.

I have been struggling to understand courage. In retrospect, I suppose I've never really thought about it deeply. Because you are my sons, and because I have become a father, I have begun to think about a topic as important as courage. Earlier, we talked about Uncle B's notion of a top 5; but consider that that notion may be a critical heuristic and shortcut, but it is by no means a panacea or first principle. Your top 5 amplify the decisions you make; they don't make your decisions for you. The choice to do what's good and hard is ultimately yours.

Lately, I have been thinking about what causes us to do the hard work of changing ourselves, regardless of who our closest friends and influences are. What causes us to choose the work to become better men? What causes us to have the humility and compassion that leads to sacrifice? What causes us to choose to walk the path of goodness instead of power? What I keep coming back to is *love*. Mere mortals will sacrifice for people and things they *love*. The same could be said for other strong emotions like anger, hate, and self-interest, but those feelings don't tend to correlate with goodness. Love is the only bonding force I have been able to find that results in goodness. Love is the thrust that carries us forward; it is what creates courageous action. Love is motion.

Let's consider what love is and how one comes to develop a real, true, enduring love.

As you have probably come to find in your lived experience, you know love when you can see or feel it, but it is hard to define specifically or authoritatively. Admittedly, I am no renowned philosopher of love, but what I do know is that those we love matter to us so much, we care about them as much or more than we care about ourselves. We volunteer to make difficult sacrifices with no strings attached, and even find joy in them, when we love.

I'm not sure love between two people can exist indefinitely if both are not willing to make sacrifices for each other. I think that is why wedding vows, at least traditional ones like those your mother and I made, talk about sickness, health, wealth, and poverty. Wedding vows are a covenant to love when it's incredibly hard. To me, love, at its essence, is the wonderful-feeling byproduct of a willingness to make sacrifices. By that definition, my sons, I love you. I love you, and always will, no matter what. I care about you, and I am willing to make sacrifices for you. That is my vow.

Love doesn't appear out of nowhere. Love is easy when it's fun, focused, or safe and expected. Choosing to act with love toward someone you have a history of loving is easy. Choosing to act with love toward someone you see on a regular basis is easy. Also, I think, when someone is good-looking. Acting with love toward a stranger is hard, especially if something you read or experienced has suggested they are untrustworthy, evil, or scary. It's hard to act with love when your heart is full of fear and anger. It's hard to act with love toward someone, stranger or not, if they're in a different time zone than you. It's *really* hard to act with love toward someone when they have wronged you or someone you love.

These examples are heavy emotional reasons that make it hard to act with love, but there are plenty of other small reasons. Maybe you're tired, hungry, hot, cold, wet, sick. It's hard to love when you're busy or have a lot on your mind, say, concerning work or money. It's harder to love when you don't have a common language or schedule with someone. Love is a choice, but sometimes that choice is harder.

Let me be clear about the kind of love I want to discuss the "how" of. I want to talk about love when it's hard, not when it's easy. You don't need my or anyone's help to act with love when the environment is joyous, warm, or celebratory. We all need help with the "unselfish, sacrificial, redemptive" love that Bishop Michael Curry talked about yesterday in the sermon he gave at the royal wedding between Prince Harry and Duchess Megan (which Robert was enjoying—mushy peas and all).

Let's get down to the trenches on this one. Let's talk about how to create thrust and put love into motion. Let's talk about unselfish, sacrificial, redemptive love. I'm still learning, but I will share the best wisdom I can.

I have been thinking and struggling over this for weeks. The longer I write these letters to you all, the more the responsibility of helping to shape your intuition and practice of goodness weighs on me. That pressure has brought the central issues of goodness into greater focus in my mind's eye. I have realized that the single, most fundamental capability in walking the path of goodness is having the courage to transform oneself. Without courage, choosing to walk the path of goodness is a fool's errand. Courageous action is the linchpin to goodness, and the linchpin of courageous action is love. For the purpose of goodness, love is tangible and tactical; it is the brass tacks of the whole enterprise.

As I've thought about love, the most important practice I can think of is listening, not just with your ears and your intellect, but the most comprehensive listening possible: with your heart, with your whole body and spirit. There is no chance of truly loving someone if you know nothing about them. Love starts with knowing something about another person's story.

When we hear that story, we find something to love about them—something about their essence and what makes them unique and special; the grace that God Himself has placed within them to shine forth. You have to understand the truth, at least a little to start, about who someone is in order to love them. There's no chance of finding something about them to love unless your heart is open to listening. Listening puts us on the journey to love because once we start to understand the compelling story, gifts, and grace everyone possesses, we are drawn to them just a little bit more than we were before. Then we learn more of their grace, and we're drawn in a little closer. And then a little closer. As we listen, we start to recognize the light in them that is as important, or more important, than our own needs. We start to value who they are and feel a genuine sense of care and concern for their well being. We see them as the same human beings we are, and without even realizing it, there comes to be love there.

When it comes to figuring out how to love, there is no bigger question than how to open up our whole body and heart and listen. The better we listen, the more its gravity draws us closer to love.

There are tips and practices that help with the mechanical aspects of listening. Before we learn to listen with our whole body and heart, we can try to listen with just our ears. Some basic techniques are to "be quiet," "confirm your understanding with questions," and "reserve judgment." A simple Google search will help you find many other tactics.

To really listen in a way that leads to a bond of love is a practice requiring more than just the mechanical aspect. Listening that creates gravity between you and someone else takes opening your heart, which is a much different enterprise

121

than what is thought of commonly as "listening."

How can we open our hearts? One reason our hearts don't open fully is that we don't have the context needed to understand someone for who they are. We often don't have an appreciation for someone else's experiences or what makes their story compelling or complex. Building context helps open our hearts to listening because we can better see and understand the other person's grace, struggles, and unique gifts. The more we understand, the more we want to learn, and the more we want to enter the halo of their human experience. I see and feel this often with other parents. I have a context of what it means to be a parent, and how difficult and exquisite it is, so when I hear a parent talk about their children, I can feel their joys and struggles intensely within *my heart*. This context helps me to do more than just listen and understand the words they are saying—it helps me to understand *them* and the incredible nuances of their story. The more I understand, the more I want to go deeper to understand them even better.

To build more context, an easy place to start is by exploring the world around you. I don't mean going to some corner of the globe, staying in a fancy hotel, and gawking at the locals from afar. I mean go somewhere unfamiliar, even uncomfortable, and embrace the different culture. That exploration does not have to be in a faraway land, though it could be. It could be anywhere outside of your backyard that forces you to experience something fundamentally new, even on the other side of our neighborhood. Go places. Be respectful. Experience new things. Meet new people. Talk to them. Stew with them. This will help you build context and open your heart to listening in a way that creates gravity and love.

Let me emphasize a subtlety here: you can't do this just by reading about it or watching it from afar. You must get in the mix to build context and experience something without a filter. Reading is valuable, but it does not replace interacting with other human beings. I am not talking about shaping your mind, but about shaping your heart and opening it up. To understand a potter, you need to get into a studio and try throwing a pot. To understand a cop, you must ride in the back of a squad car through a rough neighborhood with a bullet-proof vest on. You lose so much context when something is abstracted from primary experience. If there's a replacement for getting out there, exploring, and getting your hands dirty, I've never found it. Your instinct will often be to say "no," and avoid the discomfort that comes with novel experiences in unfamiliar places. Try to say "yes" instead.

I've also found suffering to be particularly effective in opening our hearts. Suffering kicks down the doors of our hearts, giving us no choice but to let love in. But just as easily, suffering can also rapidly close our hearts. Whether suffering opens or closes our hearts depends on how we engage with it. Suffering presents us with two important choices in how we engage with it. I'll try to explain these choices by talking about the last time I felt intense, deep suffering: when your Dada went ahead early and unexpectedly.

The first choice presented was whether to acknowledge, and let other people know, I was suffering. After my father passed, when people asked me how I was doing, I could have said something perfectly polite, but canned, like, "I'm doing as good as I can be" or "I'm hanging in there." Or I could have been honest and told them I was scared, inconsolably sad, and overwhelmed. I had the choice to suffer alone or let others in. Much of the time I wanted to suffer alone because I could stay in a state of emotional purgatory and try to be blissfully ignorant and disconnected from what I was feeling. But, in the instances I *did* let others know the truth of my suffering, it created a small opening in my heart. The people I let in tried to fill my heart with so much love, care, and compassion I could hardly believe or absorb it. That unselfish, sacrificing, redemptive love, broke my heart wide open. Suffering can powerfully and graciously open our hearts, but we can choose not to suffer alone and, instead, let love in. It is safe. Now I know, more intimately, what it feels like to have an open heart.

The second choice suffering presents is harder and perhaps more fundamental: Will we embrace the suffering or try to run from it? This choice was real and dangerous when your Dada went ahead. I used distraction as a crux. There were so many ways to avoid my suffering, to not think about it: work; hanging out with friends; perhaps even getting beers at the bar. An easy way to avoid suffering, and the pain that usually comes in tow, is to just do something else. What avoidance can't cure, delusion can. If we don't like the suffering of reality, we can build a fantasy world in our heads. If we tell ourselves, over and over, that the fantasy is true, we end up believing it. To be uncomfortably honest, a part of me created and held on to a fantasy world for months, maybe a year, after Dada died. I thought for a few days that maybe this was all a joke or that he'd come back to life in the morgue. Or maybe he would talk to me in dreams, or I would get text messages from him from the beyond if I prayed hard enough. On my weirdest days, I thought I could somehow access the multiverse or other dimensions, like in the movies or the Spider-Man comics where Peter Parker's Uncle Ben was alive in alternate versions of Earth. Our mind and heart are powerful. If we choose, we can use them to run from pain and suffering. But when we don't embrace suffering, it comes at a cost. If we close ourselves off from our suffering, we are in effect closing ourselves off from the love of others that opens us up. Living in a fantasy world keeps away the pain, temporarily at least, but it also keeps love away.

Eventually, I chose to accept reality and let others in on the secret of my suffering. Love opened up my heart, it softened me like butter softens in lukewarm water. Love poured in from your mother, our family, and our close friends, from people you call uncle and aunty. It also came from unlikely places. My friend Ava, from business school, sent me an email totally out of the blue. She worked for Facebook at the time and sent me a lesson someone from her company—Sheryl Sandberg—shared after losing her husband to cancer:

> *We don't have to be sad about being sad, we can just accept that we're sad and let it pass; we don't have to injure ourselves further by being sad about our sadness.*

Her email is an act of love I think about often; I will never forget it. When we let love in, it opens us up. Suffering also opens our hearts by creating common experiences, reminding us of our shared humanity.

I remember another email I received from someone shortly after your Dada went ahead—from one of my fraternity brothers, Eric. He wrote:

> *Neil,*

I am so sorry to hear about the loss of your father. I did not know him, but his character speaks through your tremendous drive to serve others.

I lost my brother this fall and I was surprised at what was most helpful in the grieving process. A friend of mine who had also recently lost a family member said most sincerely, "I share your pain." This made me pause. It made me adjust how I was reacting. I found that sharing it with others reduced the burden it placed on me every day. Being vulnerable to others and giving space for the grief was incredibly important to me.

I don't know what is the right method for you, but it will be a long process. It is hard to lose those we love.

Neil, I share your pain.

What is remarkable is that Eric is a fraternity brother I spent very little time with. He is several years older than me and was an upperclassman when I met him. I never lived in the fraternity house with him. I almost never hung out with him on the weekends. I hardly even conversed with him at chapter meetings. Yet, even though our friendship had been scattered a few times over a year or two, about a decade later I received this profoundly kind, compassionate, and empathetic email from him. Reading it reminds me that suffering, though tragic, is a thread that binds us in a shared human experience. When you allow yourself to experience suffering, it helps you to recognize suffering in others and understand them and love them in their defining moments. Suffering opens our heart, not just by giving others the opportunity to pour love into us, but by giving us something unshakable—a common experience of suffering with which to form a bond with others.

What awes me about suffering is that the common humanity it reminds us of creates gravity between us and people we *may not even know*, and people *we may never meet*.

You will have many opportunities to avoid suffering. When someone asks you a tough, personal question, you can choose to give deflective answers. When you are running wind sprints for athletic practice, you can choose to do the bare minimum or cut corners. When you lose me from this world, you can choose to believe it's not true. There will be many instances where you can take a path of lesser resistance and avoid suffering. I hope you do not. I hope you embrace suffering and engage with it in a way that opens your heart. I'm not suggesting, however, that you should endure senseless suffering, particularly at the hands of those who are malevolent. You should not tolerate suffering if someone is attacking you or someone else with physical, mental, or emotional abuse. What I am saying is that you should be wary of always taking a path of lesser resistance and avoiding suffering. Even though suffering is uncomfortable and often painful, it opens your heart to love and listening in a way that creates gravity. And that, my sons, creates the thrust for courageous action.

As you do more hard stuff, the more suffering you can endure. It leads to even more love and courage within your life. Suffering, love, courage, and action form a virtuous, self-reinforcing cycle. It is an important feedback loop to understand.

—

These letters I write to you often take shape over the course

127

of days or weeks. Today is June 3, 2018. It is a special day. Today, Robert, you were baptized. The morning started calmly, but just as we were leaving for church, it began to rain heavily, continuing into the afternoon. Even though this rain spoiled our plan for a celebratory barbecue with family and neighbors, it was still a wonderful day. As it happens, today's service was commemorating the celebration of Corpus Christi, which occurred earlier this week. Father Phil, the pastor, gave his homily about drinking from the cup of life, which is a concept relevant to the Eucharist, and to love and suffering because, as the story goes, Jesus suffered for our salvation. He suffered not just for Himself, but *for many*. When we drank from the cup of life, Father Phil reminded us, we get it all. We must accept both love and suffering. That's the deal with life. He challenged us to keep drinking from the cup of life, even though that choice comes with the acceptance of suffering, not just for our own life and salvation, but for others as well. This idea is consistent with our dialogue on suffering, love, courage, and action.

There is a comment Father Phil made about suffering that I had not considered. He reminded the church that Jesus did not just suffer for His friends, His allies, and His followers. He suffered and died for all, *even His enemies*. Father Phil's call to us was to do the same, that we should remember to suffer (and love) for the benefit of *all*. This is an important point. Let's consider why.

Remember that we, my sons, are engaged in this whole dialogue of letters so when we are posed with a choice, big or small, we choose based on what reflects goodness—the North Star we are trying to navigate toward. So how does suffering for, and loving, our enemies affect our ability to choose and walk the path of goodness? The affirmative case is simple. If we suffer for, listen to, and love anyone, including our enemies, that means we have more love in our hearts. We have more experiences with which to relate to others. If we can love anyone, including our enemies, what hard but important choices could we *not* have courage to make? If we can love our enemies, what courageous action can't we take? But, if we choose not to love all, we have now created a loophole, an excuse to avoid courageous action. We can now say, "I do not have to do this hard thing, even though it's the right thing, because I do not have to love my enemy." Because when we have enemies, we can call them "evil," we can treat them as "the bad guys." *Our enemies don't deserve our love and respect*, we tell ourselves. We don't have to do the hard stuff to benefit them because they're evil. If we create this excuse to not choose goodness, where does it end? We now have a slippery slope "because they're my enemy" is an ever-expandable excuse to choose power or to be cowards. The act of choosing not to suffer for, and love, all, undermines our intent to choose the path of goodness in every choice we make. If we come to a choice we don't like, we can just claim that the people it benefits are our enemies, thus eliminating our obligation and commitment to choose the path of goodness.

You may have found that the ideas in this letter were helpful, but sons, don't let my words undersell you or mislead you. Exploring the unfair and uncomfortable parts of this world is *hard*. Loving your enemies is *hard*. All these suggestions I'm making to you are *really hard.* As mortal men, your first instincts will be to resist, avoid, or outright neglect these difficult things. I am not different; I fail at this constantly, more than I let on and more than I wish I had to admit. But I will keep my word to be honest with you, even though sharing this next part makes me uneasy.

When I grew up, I was taught to fear certain types of people: Republicans; poorer people; uneducated people; Muslims— and in some cases, other racial minorities—by the culture and place I was raised in. Sure, I would like to think I have taught myself to get over these fears, but I still fail. When panhandlers approach me; for example, I still have a hard time with it, even if I know there's nothing fundamentally different about their humanity than mine. I am not proud of my prejudices, nor am I proud of how much more open I know my heart could be, but isn't. I should say, I know I need to continue putting in the work—getting older and grayer are not excuses for not continuing to open my heart. I suppose that's why I'm telling you this, so you aren't afraid to choose the work, so you aren't afraid to be uncomfortable. At times, choosing the work will be exceptionally hard—to the point where every limb in your body is telling you to avoid opening your heart, or suffering, or loving everyone. This will shape you into a person who chooses the work and walks the path of goodness. This is as true for you as it is for me.

And, my sons, even though you will fail like I fail, keep going. It will be hard in the moment, but you won't regret it, not for a second.

Love,
Papa

* * *

13

Convictions

**When the tough gets going, and the luring songs of power,
comfort, convenience, and sloth are calling to you, the
deep foundations of your soul, where your convictions
are rooted, will hold the line.**

June 19, 2018

My Sons,

One well-known and successful company, at the time I am writing this letter, is Google. Hopefully they will still be around by the time you read this. I am not particularly captivated by Google's core business of search and advertising. What I have been intrigued by, however, is a unit of their organization called X, which takes a radical approach to their work, compared to most companies. At X, they go after moonshots. What this means is that they do two things: (1) they go after huge problems of major consequence; and (2) they try to make massive improvements from the status quo

131

rather than making something incrementally better. When humans put a man on the moon, it was a seemingly impossible challenge and a major leapfrog to the status quo of the day, hence the moniker "moonshots" and "moonshot thinking."

Famously, X applies "10x" thinking to their work. They try to make the status quo ten times better than what it currently is. So, if X was working on something, they would want to make it ten times better than status quo. If they were working on something like drug discovery technology, they would want to make it ten times better. By virtue of trying to make a 10x improvement, they work on really hard stuff (i.e., not bricks and pens) because hard, consequential problems are where a 10x improvement over status quo is both possible and worth the effort.

What I find compelling about 10x thinking is that it forces us to approach a problem in a fundamentally different way because, to make a 10x improvement, a team must break current day trade-offs and constraints. Let me give you an example I think about a lot these days because of my job: reducing murders.

In the past year, Detroit had about 300 murders. If we, at the police department, were to reduce murders by 10%, we would have to reduce them by 30, which is about 2-3 fewer murders within each of the 12 precincts within the Detroit Police Department (DPD). If each precinct only had to prevent three murders, that wouldn't *seem* hard. In that sort of scenario, each DPD precinct could just do what it's doing a bit better. At least for a while, we wouldn't have to change our strategies fundamentally. Improving something, especially murder rates, by 10% is not easy, but it certainly doesn't, on its face, require a fundamentally different crime prevention strategy. But let's apply 10x thinking instead. In this example, that would mean having homicides become ten times lower, which would imply going from 300 homicides per year to 30 homicides per year. Going from 300 homicides in Detroit to 30, for a cop, would be like rewriting the laws of gravity. We can't just do what we do a little better to improve by that order of magnitude. We would have to do something extremely unorthodox and completely rethink the problem from first principles. Radical change requires radical action.

Clearly, applying 10x thinking leads us to consider options that seem impossible; it leads to projects that push your mind and body to the edge. Moonshot projects are ones where the team should expect to fail—and fail many times before they *maybe* succeed. They require difficult sacrifices, relentless willpower, and unflinching creativity. These 10x projects are so hard that a reasonable person would probably question why anyone would be interested in working for X or attempting a moonshot of their own. But that's why X doesn't work on bricks and pens, they work on projects of tremendous impact and consequence.

Doing really hard stuff, like moonshot projects, doesn't just require fundamentally different approaches, it requires a fundamentally different mindset and convictions—deep ones—because without believing the work you are doing is tremendously important, why would you waste your time trying to do the impossible? Without convictions and a deep sense of purpose, even the most talented people aren't often courageous enough to try for the moon. So, let's talk about convictions and apply what we learn to courage.

Perhaps the easiest place to start is by talking about what convictions are not, rather than what they are. Convictions are not facts. Facts are true observations about the world. That water is made up of hydrogen and oxygen is a fact. That humans need to breathe oxygen to survive is a fact. That Shakespeare wrote plays in English is a fact. Believing it's possible to reduce homicides in Detroit from 300 per year to 30 per year is not a fact. Convictions are not facts; they fall into the domain of opinion.

Let's build a ladder here because not all opinions are convictions—there's a difference between levels of opinions: general opinions; beliefs; and convictions. In the way I mean them here, the difference between general opinions and beliefs is that general opinions are descriptive (describing how the world or state of being is) and beliefs are normative (articulating an opinion on how the world or state of being should be). "Orange juice is the best juice" is a general opinion on a beverage I prefer. "Orange juice should be available at every soda fountain" is a belief about the way I think the world should distribute beverages. The former is descriptive; the latter is normative.

Usually, general opinions like "I like orange juice" are easier to discuss and negotiate in a community of people because the audience can just ask me to verify that I like orange juice. Additionally, the fact that I like orange juice doesn't have an immediate implication for other people. The fact that I like orange juice puts you under no obligation to like orange juice. This makes differences in opinion relatively easy to discuss and reconcile in most cases. General opinions, relatively speaking, are benign.

The belief that "orange juice should be available at every soda fountain" is different. If that belief were carried out, it would have implications for other people and organizations. If my belief were codified into law, it would require restaurants to purchase a lot of orange juice concentrate. Schools and beverage distributors may need to acquire lots of new equipment for dispensing or refrigerating orange juice. The requirement to provide access to orange juice may cause soda sellers to stop carrying other juices, angering people who prefer apple, cranberry, or tomato.

Because beliefs are normative, they affect others when acted upon. Unlike general opinions, which are merely descriptive, beliefs lead to bigger disagreements and are usually more difficult to reconcile in a community. Beliefs, more than general opinions, can lead to conflict and sometimes even violence.

You'll probably find that most people, more or less, think that beliefs and convictions are the same thing. Except that convictions are beliefs that are "really, really strong." I'll admit that, up until about four hours ago, when I started writing this letter to you, I would have been one of those people. The distinction between beliefs and convictions I have in my mind is along the same lines as "really, really strong," but I hope that by being more specific it will help us learn something important about courage.

I have lots of beliefs; someday you will too. Your mother has lots of beliefs and so will all your friends. And for me, your mom, and all those other people, many of those beliefs may be strong. But beliefs, even strong ones, are inexpensive in a way. You can develop strong beliefs and even express them verbally, or on the Internet, easily. These days, you don't even have to say them out loud or in person, you can just post them on any number of internet-based mediums. Today, just as it's been for decades or perhaps centuries, it's possible to hold a strong belief without having to give up anything or bear any sort of cost. As is often said, *talk is cheap*. Lots of people, myself included, talk big game about things they believe. But very few beliefs are ones someone will bear actual costs for—social, financial, or otherwise. A person may have a strong belief that the world should accept all religions and be more pluralistic, but will that person sacrifice the time to read religious texts from across different traditions? Will they be willing to attend an interfaith dialogue their parents disapprove of? Will they open their home to a refugee seeking asylum from religious persecution? Maybe, maybe not. Someone may strongly believe that more people should receive housing subsidies, but will they welcome mixed-income housing units being built in their neighborhood? Someone may strongly believe pollution from automobiles is destroying the environment, but will they leave their car at home and ride a bicycle to work?

This is how I distinguish a belief from a conviction: a conviction is a belief for which the person is willing to sacrifice. Holding a strong belief you are willing to bear a cost for (facing scrutiny or perhaps intimidation), in real life, is uncommon and special.

And that, my sons, is why convictions are central to courage. If you have found something you have convictions for, you can lean on them when things get hard and you're wavering. It creates momentum and a force of thrust that will carry you forward. When the tough gets going, and the luring songs of power, comfort, convenience, and sloth are calling to you, the deep foundations of your soul, where your convictions are rooted, will hold the line.

A simple example Will Smith uses in his memoir, *Will*, explains this. Nobody wants to run at 5a.m., and nobody wants to turn down a plate of cheese fries, but we know the right things for our body. Though we know this, it is still easy to cave to the comfort of our bed or the taste of a cheesy, fried potato. This is where conviction comes in. I, myself, believe in being healthy, but it's not a conviction. I desire to be strong and attractive, but that desire is not enough for me to put on my trainers and run on a Sunday afternoon when it's cold outside. Health, strength, and looking good are things I want for myself, but I'm not willing to make sacrifices for them. My conviction comes from losing my father so early in life. I sacrifice sloth and French fries to maintain a diet and exercise regimen because I have to be around long enough and be healthy enough to see you three grow up. I don't want to be tired and sore; I want to be able to roll on the ground and play Legos, or lightsabers, or whatever it is, with you. I want to be able to get on the floor and play with *your children* if you become fathers. I want to be around much longer for you than my father was able to be for me. I am determined—convicted—on this. I lost my father way too early in life to poor health. I absolutely cannot let that happen to *you*, so I am able to make sacrifices around diet and exercise that I wouldn't have made otherwise.

You must be wondering: *How?* As I normally do when I'm stuck, I asked your mother. I shared my theory on what makes a belief a conviction with her. Then I asked her something like, "How does a person end up with convictions?" Immediately, she said something simple and wise: "A person ends up with convictions when their beliefs are 'reinforced through experience.'" That's the key! You must do more than just ponder what your beliefs and convictions are. You must live through them, feel them, *breathe* them.

If you believe good food is important, grow a garden, or learn to cook and see what it feels like. If you believe that all we need is love, show your love and see what it feels like. If you believe nobody should be hungry, share your lunch and see what it feels like. Go out there, live, and give your beliefs the chance to be *reinforced with experiences.*

As you live out your beliefs, some of them will fizzle out and you won't sacrifice for them again. For other beliefs, when you actually live them out and put them into practice, something will happen. You will feel something profound wash over you. Your experience will reinforce the belief and mold it into a conviction. I always kind of believed that diet and exercise mattered, but once your Dada went ahead, my experience of grieving him reinforced my belief and turned it into a conviction. If you want to find your convictions, then live your life, do something, listen to the wisdom of experience with your heart, and see the patterns in what sticks.

You do not need to go far and wide or have an expensive, structured, or highly controlled adventure to go out and live. Life comes to your doorstep. Just let it in, you don't have to go looking for it.

Your granddad and mom talk about "inflection points." These are the big moments. The gut check times. The moments in your life that cause inflections in your trajectory and precede a change in direction. These moments are often brief, maybe a day or week or month, but it's as if you end up living ten years' worth of life in those moments. Inflection points are experiences that have a disproportionate impact on reinforcing your beliefs. They forge beliefs into convictions.

When I was 13, your Cha Cha Nakul went ahead. I remember hearing about it. I was just about to start high school and had some friends over hanging out. It took months for me to truly understand what had happened and what it meant, but it was an inflection point. Nakul died of dengue fever. He was the first case in the area around Gwalior, your Dada and Dadi's hometown in India. The healthcare system in Gwalior, where he was living at the time, was unprepared. They didn't have the ability to treat dengue fever. Even as a teenager, this is something I could not fathom. (Human civilization knows how to treat dengue fever. It's serious business, but nobody should have to die from it—we now KNOW BETTER.) Inflection point. After his death, my beliefs about government turned into a conviction: institutions, especially governments, have a moral duty to be managed and operated well because they are the best and sometimes last line of defense between life, death, and senseless human suffering. I had always gravitated toward social studies and government classes in school, but Nakul's death turned that belief in the importance and duty of government into a *conviction*. That conviction drove me to serve in government, even when plenty of people I knew questioned my choice.

When your Dada went ahead, it shook me. It still shakes me. The life path I was on was great, but I had taken for granted that I could just focus on my career and get back to family stuff later. Then he was gone, and I was alone. His passing, and your mother's influence, turned my belief that family is important into the conviction of *family first*. Inflection point.

In a way, I have had an uncommon life. I have worked on hundreds, maybe thousands, of teams through school, work, and community. I have worked in dozens of different organizations. I have traveled all around the country as a consultant. I've experienced environments of extreme wealth and poverty in my travels around the world and around the country. I have met people who work on the shop floor and in the boardroom. In high school and college, I hung out with pretty much every clique and group at one point or another. On the aforementioned business trip to rural Kentucky (and Tennessee), visiting soap factories, put honestly, I had expected everyone to be a dumb, racist hillbilly to some degree, but I was wrong. I met some of the most compassionate, kindest people I've ever encountered in my life. Upon meeting one of the plant managers at a factory, I could tell I was in the presence of a tremendous leader as I walked with him through the plant. He was the sort of guy that wouldn't benefit from an Ivy League MBA because there is nothing a school could teach him about leadership. My expectations were totally wrong. Inflection point.

That trip was the experience that finally crystallized and reinforced a set of beliefs I picked up in all my life and travels: *I've met good people.* Across geographies and ages and races and backgrounds, I've met people with talent who have something to contribute. All those little moments have shifted my beliefs into a conviction that it is a moral duty to find the best in others and help them share their gifts with the world. That means I can't talk badly about anyone, even people at work who annoy me. My conviction that we need to find the best in others compels me to find compassion for others, coach others, and elevate others, including outcasts under scrutiny. I'm a mortal man, so I'm not perfect at honoring this conviction, but I am compelled to keep trying and to keep becoming better at it.

I wish that was all there was to it, for convictions at least, but that is only half of it. Experiences don't reinforce your beliefs on their own. It's not that easy. You must absorb them. You must process them. You must internalize them. You can't just live your experiences. In order to form convictions, you must reflect on them. To internalize your experiences and have them reinforce your beliefs into convictions, you must ask the harder questions and put in the emotional labor those questions require. Surface-level questions (general opinions, such as what you like and dislike, what went well and what didn't) are okay and a decent place to start. Questions that feel like cliches and don't tap into strong emotions are not sufficient for internalizing your experiences and letting them shift your beliefs into convictions.

The next level down are questions regarding your strengths and weaknesses. They help you understand how you fit into the world; that's important, but it's still not deep enough to reveal your convictions. The hard questions you need to ask are ones you feel in your body when you hear them. It's as if your corporeal self gets activated and primed to reveal a secret. Questions, like the following, are hard; they go deep: What really matters to you? What is moral? What are you willing to sacrifice? What's intolerable? What am I feeling about this, really? What does everyone deserve? What do we owe others? Figure out how to ask yourself these questions and answer them honestly.

When I was around age 12, I had a spiral notebook. It had colorful yellow, blue, and green vertical stripes down the front. I called it the Question Book. I made a list of questions and wrote them on the inside cover of the notebook. Then I would pick one question and place it at the top of one of the pages and start to write; sometimes, for hours. I pushed myself not to bullshit. I don't think another living soul has seen that notebook. Even at that young age, morsels of my convictions started to reveal themselves because I reflected on what was happening around me, what I was feeling and why, and I went for hard questions that took something out of me. Writing is what I do to reflect, but it need not be your medium.

You could be a writer, but you could also be a painter. Or a rapper. Or a poet. Or a musician and song writer. Or a podcaster or a comedian. Maybe you're the friend who gets everyone around a campfire to talk. Maybe your channel to internalize your experiences is meditation or prayer. You each have to figure out the mediums of reflection that work best for you. I promise to help you figure it out. It's hard to even start reflecting. I'm lucky I have had a lot of people in my life—teachers, family, camp counselors, friends, and others—show me the ropes. I will do my best to do the same for you.

In life, we try and fail often. Sometimes we achieve goals and dreams; other times, we don't. It's hard. But my hope is that all we have talked about will give you a foundation to start. Even if I haven't given you all the answers, I hope to at least have provided a footing for the hard stuff as you walk the path of goodness.

My biggest and most important moonshot is the dream of our family. Your mother and I are shooting for the moon. The hardest thing I have ever done is marry your mother and try to be a good husband; then, bring you, our children, and our pup, Riley, together and build a family. Building a family has required me to change routines, relationships, and my priorities. It has required tremendous sacrifices, both from me and your mother. We have given up sleep, freedom, and money. The moonshot of family has revealed to me, brutally, how selfish I still am and that I want to be better. Being a husband

and father humbled me. But I say this with absolute certitude and the deepest conviction: being a husband to your mother and a father to you is the most important work of my life and the greatest gift of my life. My dreams are fulfilled. Only becoming one with God Himself could be more special. Our family is my greatest sacrifice and my deepest, most precious joy. *Family first*.

I give you the sincerest blessing a father can give to his children. I wish and pray that you will be able to do something this hard and joyous in your own life. I pray for you to all have the gift of family in your life. I pray that you will cherish the gift of brotherhood. Your life, and navigating its joys and sacrifices, will be hard. The path of goodness is hard. I hope and I pray these ideas are lights that guide and comfort you along the way.

Love,
Your Papa

✳ ✳ ✳

14

Persistence

We will never be perfect; we will never be gods.

November 3, 2018

My Sons,

Everything I have written, thus far, has been to help you to achieve a singular purpose: to do something hard. The idea is that by having the capability of doing hard things, you will be more willing to choose the work and become more capable of walking the path toward goodness. If your character were a muscle, everything we have discussed could be compared to sharing ideas with you for doing the first workout of a difficult weightlifting regiment: squats; clean jerks; and the bench press, for strengthening. Our discussions would be analogous to telling you why it's important to exercise, how to get yourself to the gym, and how to do the first, difficult workout. Thus far, we've only talked about how to get to and through day one.

And you've done it! In this metaphorical gym, you've done

your first workout. This is not trivial. Doing one "workout" to strengthen your character is not easy to do intentionally, even once. Now, we must train consistently to build more muscular strength. The process of building curiosity and courage would be a test of any man's mettle. Because we are fallible, mortal men, your successes and sheer exhaustion from acting with curiosity and courage will make you believe you are done, that you've had enough, that you're done growing and that you cannot be, nor need to be, a better man tomorrow than you are today. You might try to fool yourself into thinking you don't have to choose the work or walk the path of goodness any longer. Perhaps, even worse, your successful attempts to practice courage may tempt you to believe: *I am already a better man than my peers, why bother doing more?*

I have had all of these thoughts before, but remember: WE WILL NEVER BE DONE. We are not gods, my sons, we are mortal men. We must keep choosing the work required to walk the path of goodness. If our character muscles aren't growing stronger, they are suffering from atrophy. Therefore, we need an additional core capability to push us forward: persistence; a concept that goes beyond the idea of consistency; habit; or even discipline. Nothing in the world can take the place of persistence. The notion of persistence is familiar to me because it is a core concept in the teachings of my fraternity, Phi Gamma Delta. When I was a college freshman starting to adjust to life in Ann Arbor, that first fall, I spent many Wednesday evenings at the Fiji house, as a pledge, learning the principles and operations of the fraternity. One of the first things we had to do was commit the following quote to memory, which were the words of one of our Fiji brothers, President Calvin Coolidge:

145

Nothing in this world can take the place of persistence.
Talent will not; nothing is more common than unsuccess-
ful men with talent. Genius will not; unrewarded genius
is almost a proverb. Education will not; the world is
full of educated derelicts. Persistence and determination
alone are omnipotent. The slogan 'Press On' has solved
and will always solve the problems of the human race.

My sons, I have found this to be true. Everything in the world that really matters: marriage; parenthood; citizenship; profound works of art or science; goodness; life itself, comes through persistence. There are no overnight successes that happen from talent, genius, or education alone, goodness included. To create good things in this world, we must persist through challenge after challenge. If we want to become better men today than we were yesterday, we must act with persistence. Why? If we feel like we haven't reached our full potential for goodness, the answer to "why persistence" is easy. There is a greater ability to grow purer of heart and more benevolent in our intentions and actions. If we feel we can become better—more good—it's easy to justify why persistence matters because we're *not done yet.* But what if we feel we are done, like we have become as good as we can be? What if we feel like we've chosen the work, walked the path of goodness, and reached the end? Or even more realistically, what if we feel we can't grow anymore? Even if we know we are still not fully "good" people, what if we feel like, no matter what we do, we cannot grow further, even if we tried?

If you have become so supremely good that you literally cannot be more good, I cannot argue that. If you have become so perfect you are mistaken for a god, then I concede that persistence isn't a capability worth developing or putting into action. But we are mortal men—we will never be perfect; we will never be gods.

But what if you think you're *good enough?* What if you feel you've walked far enough? If you recall the basis of my rationale for choosing the work required to walk the path of goodness, the essence of the argument was that if we live in a community instead of the state of nature, the tradeoff for the prosperity and stability that comes with a growing society is corruption. If we have vulnerabilities to corruption, which corrode the functioning of a community, there are two general approaches to deal with it: (1) create more rules (institutions); or (2) create more good people (trust). We discussed that the most straightforward way to create more good people is to be good men ourselves. Our actions have ripple effects. Our actions influence others. Our actions are what nudge the culture to be more good. The goodness we exude in our actions matters. What I have realized is that our struggle with culture also nudges the culture toward goodness. When I tell you about how I'm struggling but persisting with keeping a cool temperament as a parent, or when I write a blog post about how I'm struggling but persisting to deal with grief, people respond to that struggle to persist. Our example of goodness nudges the culture, but so does our example of persistence.

Truthfully, I don't believe I will ever be such a good person that I could take a break for the rest of my life. The older I get, the more I feel I have more room to grow. But for discussion's sake, let's say we have actually achieved that "good enough" state. Even then, we must persist because our persistence, as much as our example of goodness, nudges the culture to be better. More likely you will start to feel, not that you've grown enough, but that you can't grow further. This is perhaps the *most important* time to persist. These are the real-life moments, when our mettle is tested, that we need to lean into our capability to persist the most. Let me tell you this: I've often doubted I could continue to grow. I have thought that I had gone too far in my ways to try something different.

I often think about a conversation I mentioned before, the one I had with my father, probably two years before he went ahead, when I was asking him the simple, sincere questions about his life. Your Dada struggled tremendously throughout his life, and whether he could have or not, he never took his eye off the here and now. Probably because his life had been so unstable for so long, he never felt he had the luxury to step back and understand the bigger picture of his life and the deeper feelings in his heart. A sense of resigned remorse came over him because, he said, he believed too much time had passed, that it was too late for him to change. I remember the regret on his face and how the pressure of the air around us seemed to change so vividly. It was a profoundly sad, but unforgettable moment. I hope I said something caring and empathetic around the kitchen island that day. I've reflected on this difficult situation of feeling like I can't change, even if I wanted to. First, I've thought about it in terms of sunk costs. Everything we have done in our lives prior to today is a sunk cost. We can't change it. We shouldn't make decisions based on sunk costs because they're already done. We don't have to throw good money after bad money. The same is true of our actions: we get a new start every day. We don't have to continue the trends of past practice just because we have done it for a long time. We can move in a new direction today if we want to. I like the way Seth Godin thinks about sunk costs. Roughly put, they are gifts from our past selves, and we can choose to accept or reject them. We're not beholden to our past actions, nor must we reject them completely. What we choose to do and whether we choose to change is precisely that—a choice.

Secondly, regardless of whether we choose to or not, we will change. We are changing all the time. Every new day, the world around us changes and we have new experiences. Every new day, we acquire new information and feedback on our actions. These things change us, even just a little. The way I figure it, if we are going to change anyway, why not be intentional about it and change by choice?

Finally, I have thought a lot about changing the frame of what success is. It can be incredibly demotivating if you feel that, when you change, the fruits of your efforts won't matter, if you feel like you can never be great, if it doesn't feel worth it to be average, even if you are better than before. These are yardstick problems. In these scenarios, the reference point of what success is (the yardstick), frames the change as futile. But it's not that the change is futile, it's that the yardstick makes it seem that way. At some point in the past 15 years, I have tried to reframe my life with a gentler, more generous yardstick. I try very hard to no longer measure what I am trying to do based on external measures. I simply think, *will this make me a better man tomorrow than I am today? Am I 1% better a man than I was yesterday?*

It is obvious why persistence matters. We should keep trying to become better. Even virtuous people have reason to persist in their efforts to keep becoming better because their continued effort to transform increases their impact on the

149

culture, bending it toward goodness. And we can change for the better, even if we don't think we can. Our persistence, at the end of the day, is a sacrifice and a gift to the culture. We should not just persist when it's "worth it." We should persist because we *can*.

As I write this, I am beginning to see this may be irrational for someone who makes decisions based on the principles of utility maximization. Why would we persistently make sacrifices? Especially when the people who will benefit are people of the future that we may never know, and not us? Why should we persist in our efforts toward goodness only because we can?

When I look at you or your mother, what was once irrational is no longer irrational. When I look at you, or hold you, or play with you, or rock you to sleep, I feel something I can't explain, a feeling that turns off the rational homo economicus part of my brain. It makes me want to do anything and everything for the rest of my life to be better. Why? So your generation, or your children's generation, or their children's generation, on down, can live in a better world. It's recursive thinking. You matter to me. And your children and their friends will matter to you, so they matter to me. And so on for generations and generations until that expands to every person who lives after I will live. It is my love for our family, friends, and this ever-expanding tree of relationships that makes me want to persist. How could I not? Every day I have a chance to nudge the culture in a better direction.

Boys, on this question of "why persistence," there's no appeal I can make to your rational self-interest. I have no answer to the question: "What's in it for me?" But I would say this: If you are lucky enough to have a family that loves you—

blood-related or not—and a strong, unconditional love for something bigger than yourselves … even people you will never know, you will be the luckiest of men. If you are so lucky, "because you can" will be reason enough for persistence toward goodness.

Love,
Papa

* * *

III

2019

15

Getting Out of Your Own Way

With faith, we can focus all our energy on pressing forward.

March 22, 2019

My Dear Sons,

As you know, boys, I like to write. Writing is a different sort of task. In signing a sales receipt at a restaurant or filling out a health questionnaire at the doctor's office, it might require the writing of words, but it isn't writing. Receipts and questionnaires have a structure that is already pre-defined for us—all we have to do is fill in the blanks. Most of the thinking, on things like receipts and questionnaires, has already been done for us. Starting with a blank page is different because, in addition to having to do all the thinking, you also bear all the risk. When you start with a blank page, you cannot blame someone else if what you write is crummy; it's all on you. So, what happens? We find reasons to let it stay blank. We think we have to find the "perfect" thing to say. We think we have to find the best pen and notebook for the job. We remember the sweeping we forgot to do or the email we forgot to respond to and think it's more important than our blank page. The thing is, we don't *need* to think or have the perfect thing, we just need to *start writing*. We think writer's block is real, but it's not. It's just a symptom of what's really going on: getting in our own way by making excuses. Here's one way to change this: use brute force and willpower to press on. The problem is: that strategy is costly. Expending your will power to persist through excuses is draining. It steals your mental energy. It's an approach with some merit, but it has its limits. Willpower is important, but, on its own, it's not a sustainable strategy. Other strategies are possible, but we must better understand why we make excuses before we can put those strategies into practice.

Making excuses is, unfortunately, easy to do. Once you start paying attention, you will start to see yourself making excuses everywhere. I have made excuses in many ways and forms. I've not applied for jobs and admissions into schools because I thought I would get rejected. I have padded deadlines on projects so I would have some cushion. It took me a long time to ask for your mom's phone number, and even longer to ask her out on a date. There have been house projects, like fixing a faucet, repairing plaster, sealing radiator valves, etc., I haven't done because of different excuses. Plenty of small reasons, like laziness and disorganization, come into play. But looking back at all the excuses I have made over the years, especially the big stuff, it all comes down to stories.

Plain and simple, we care about stories. We care about the stories people tell about us and that we tell ourselves about who we are. These stories affect what we believe we can do, how others treat us and, ultimately, how we feel. These stories add up and affect how we act.

Excuses are a way for us to influence the stories other people tell about us and the stories we tell about ourselves. They also protect us from stories we are afraid of. The way excuses work is simple. Say you need to do something hard. Because that thing is hard; for example, committing to a healthier diet or keeping your house clean, you think you might fail. If you fail, you might now have to contend with these stories, whether self-imposed or imposed by others, about your "being a failure." So instead of risking doing something that will make you feel like a failure, you make an excuse instead. You say things like, "my diet isn't *that* bad" or "I'm too busy to worry about having a clean room now." If you make the excuse before you do the hard thing, you can now NOT do the hard thing. This takes failure off the table because you can't fail at something you are not doing. If you make the excuse *after* the fact, and you had "failed," you can save face a little bit by deflecting the blame and failure away from you and onto the object of the excuse. When you think about it, excuses are a rational response to the pressure of stories and managing their impact on our thoughts and actions. But, if we don't make excuses, what is our alternative? There are three strategies I can think of: (1) we can reframe how we see ourselves; (2) we can try to author our own story, or (3) we can try to detach our identity from our stories. No single strategy is sufficient on its own; rather, it's best to experiment with all three approaches.

Over the course of my life, I have cared a lot about how other people see me. I didn't realize it was happening, but caring about the expectations of others made me evaluate my worth and my life based on what other people believed and thought was important. This focus on others' expectations led to a particular pressure: I wanted to tell myself the story that other people liked me and approved of how I was living my life. And because of that pressure, I made excuses that made me act outside my values or preferences, like: "I really do think it's a good idea to go to business school," or, "I really do like watching sports all the time," or, "I would like to remodel our house enough to be selected for the bi-annual home tour." The pressure of other people's expectations made me pretend to believe things I actually didn't. Because of this, I didn't persist in doing hard things, such as figuring out what I cared about as a vocation, pursuing interests I actually cared about, or tempering my greed for more money that could have gone into house projects. So, the goal is clear: to see ourselves through our own eyes and live our lives based on our own standards. If we do this, we remove some of the pressure.

How you start to see yourself through your own eyes instead of others' is quite simple. First, identify the expectation you feel you are supposed to be meeting, then replace it with your own. That's an abstract concept, so let me give you a few examples that I have found useful.

Clayton Christensen, a well-known business strategy professor at Harvard Business School, posed a question: "How will you measure your life?" This question forces deep reflection and takes on a difficult challenge: setting a philosophy for how you live your life and make meaning of it.

Warren Buffett has a related concept, which brings forth the question of how you measure your life: *inner scorecards* vs. *outer scorecards*. People fall into one of two categories: people who have inner scorecards (who live their lives by standards they set for themselves) and people who have outer scorecards (who live their lives by standards set by others). What Warren Buffet, many other thinkers, and I personally have found is that life is much better when you live based on an inner scorecard. What I would add is, when you live with an inner scorecard, it's also easier to persist through difficult things because we're less fickle about goals we have convictions about.

It is not complicated to set your own inner scorecard, but it does take intention and time. I learned an exercise from Kathy MacDonald, a coach I had as a graduate student at the Ross School of Business, that helped me discover the beginnings of my own inner scorecard. I revisit it around every 12 to 18 months… Draw the following table on a piece of paper. Take your time to fill it out honestly.

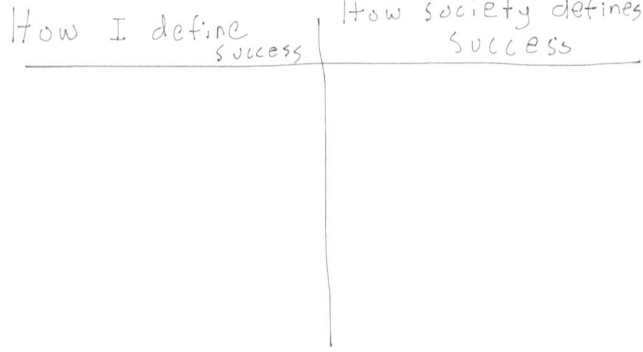

Doing this exercise can help you to devise a simple way to

conceptualize the result you intend to create with your life.

Warren Buffet's rule of thumb is to ask if the people he loves love him back. I'm still refining my own inner scorecard, but it essentially boils down to asking: *Am I a better man—husband, father, and citizen—than I was yesterday?*

What I have found to be especially difficult is finding the head space to have independent thinking. To be honest enough to create your own inner scorecard, you have to get everyone's expectations out of your head for a while. Everyone else's expectations come at you, from all directions, all the time. There's advertising everywhere. Social networks are in your pocket all the time. There are routines embedded throughout your day that trigger memories and experiences that remind you of other people's expectations, like looking in the mirror, weighing yourself, or even calling your mother on the phone. What I've found that works is seeking solitude. Be alone for a while; put your phone and computer away. You don't have to go to Walden Pond and disappear into nature (though you could). You can find solitude in a crowded room. You just have to turn off awareness of your surroundings. Solitude is well worth the practice. If you seek and find solitude and commit to it, it's almost inevitable that you will go down the path of contemplation. You must also constantly practice and reinforce the application of your inner scorecard. Your mom has helped me put this into practice over the last few months. We have been experimenting with a daily ritual, where your mom and I ask each other three questions, usually around the dinner table or on the couch after we have read you a story and tucked you in:

- What were your highs?

- What were your lows?
- What were you proud of?

The trick is to not answer these questions mindlessly, especially "what you were proud of." When we first started making this part of our routine, your mom encouraged me to think about the answer through the lens of an inner scorecard, rather than an outer one; meaning, I started evaluating my day, not by the accomplishments I had at work and whether I was "winning," but rather by the sort of man—husband, father, citizen—I was and whether I was being a man of good character. Answering this question, intentionally, with this frame, helped me to be honest about whether I was living out my inner scorecard. This practice reprogrammed my brain and how I see myself. My stress levels started to fall, but more importantly, by forcing me to think through the lens of my inner scorecard every day, it reprogrammed how I view the world, so my default viewpoint is starting to be based on an inner scorecard rather than an outer one.

Another reason we make excuses is because we are unsure of ourselves. When we don't understand ourselves, we don't know how our efforts will translate into achieving our goals and we can't hear other people tell us we have strengths. Your Dada used to tell me I was a capable person. Constantly hearing this from my father has been a foundational source of confidence in my life. However, I realized in the past year or so that I needed to discover for myself what those capabilities are and understand why. I need to be able to write my own story. If we write our own stories, we feel less likely to fail, or like we can figure out any challenge we come across. When we feel we can write our own stories, we don't have to make excuses because we know we can lean on our strengths and write our own triumphant or redemptive ending. To develop self-authorship, we need to understand our specific, uniquely gifted strengths—our superpowers—and how they fit into the world around us, through a practice of introspection.

Here are a few exercises I have found useful. One is the " reflected best self exercise." Here, you select a wide variety of people (10-20 is good) who know you from different aspects of your life, and ask them, nicely, with lots of gratitude, to give you 2-3 examples of when they thought you were at your best. Ask them to be as detailed about what they saw, why they thought you were at your best in those moments, and what strengths they see in you. Then, read what everyone shares with you and connect the dots and determine the patterns you see. Another approach is to use an instrument to help you determine your strengths. The one I like most is from the Gallup company; it is called CliftonStrengths. Unlike other surveys (e.g., the Myers-Briggs Type Indicator), I find it to be more focused on strengths rather than personality or disposition. The strengths are also specific, rather than a four-category classification, which is helpful. Finally, you can process your own experiences. Think about times you have achieved your best and reflect on what underlying strengths allowed you to succeed. Dr. Peet (you may remember her from when I was writing about curiosity) has a great technique called Generative Interviewing, which truly brought this to life for me.

In a generative interview, you share three stories with your partner about when you felt at your best. You try to tell the story in detail and your partner asks you questions with radical curiosity. Then, your partner shares the connections they saw across the stories and the specific superpower unique to you that they reveal.

But there is a danger here. There is a fine line between the confidence that comes from self-authorship and the hubris that comes from self-centeredness. The truth is, you may be the leading character of your own story, but ours is not the only story that matters. Our individual stories intertwine and weave together with the stories of others, like our top 5, our family and friends, our neighbors, and even the stories of perfect strangers. We shouldn't forget that we are one story in a beautiful symphony of many, many others.

The reason this matters goes way back to our discussion about tribes and the corruption problem. If we believe we are better or more important than everyone else, we start to believe ours is the only story that matters. This puts us at risk of falling for the temptations of power because we end up believing we are more capable of handling power and that we need it more badly than others. We believe we're deserving of special treatment and that the rules don't apply to us. Starting to think with hubris is a dangerous, slippery slope. We can easily fall into our lust for power and fool ourselves into thinking it's all for the sake of the good, that we are exceptional, and that we can wield that power more responsibly than others. The remedy for hubris is humility. Humility opens our eyes to the capabilities and stories of others.

I have just shared with you my insights on how to discover your superpowers. You can use these same techniques to discover the superpowers in others. Once you do that, for every person you meet, you will find a reason to be humble. Everyone in this world is special and has a story worth knowing. The sum total of human potential is unfathomably big. And even more awesome is the inspiration and meaning every story brings. I've seen the extraordinary in the people your mom has started to know at work, who have cared for their ill and aging parents. I've seen the extraordinary in my colleagues in gang violence prevention who were incarcerated for murder, found redemption and renewal, and chose to spend their efforts helping youth avoid the cycle of violence. I've seen the extraordinary in the flight attendants who help children navigate foreign airports when flying alone, building uncommon kindness for people they just met. Our neighbors, the Eldreds, are everyday people, but they have found a way to travel the world and make deep friendships across the globe. The world we live in, my sons, is an extraordinary place, if you're willing to see it. When you start to look for the extraordinary, you can't help but realize you are a small part of it, with an extraordinary contribution to make and an extraordinary story to share.

My sons, there is so much I already see in each of you—even at your very young ages. You, all three of you, are very capable people—each extraordinary in different ways. Your mother and I will help you learn and understand these extraordinary gifts for yourselves.

The third strategy for managing the pressure of our stories is non-attachment. There is an assumption that we need to be attached to, and care about, stories told about us and stories we tell ourselves—but must we? If we removed the attachment, we could have energy back to keep moving forward. The only way to fully get out of our own way is to detach from the need to control our stories. But how?

I have been exploring theology and moral philosophy more in the past five years. Luckily, we have a long tradition in thinking about non-attachment from our Hindu roots. There is an easy path to non-attachment: surrender, then relinquish all ownership of the results of your actions and attach them to God. If the results in my life are on God, the story of my life is on God, and I am free from attachment to my story. From there, I can go on without feeling the need to make excuses. Swami Vivekananda puts it well here:

> *Here are the two ways of giving up all attachment. The one is for those who do not believe in God, or in any outside help. They are left to their own devices; they have simply to work with their own will, with the powers of their mind and discrimination, saying, "I must be non-attached". For those who believe in God there is another way, which is much less difficult. They give up the fruits of work unto the Lord; they work and are never attached to the results. Whatever they see, feel, hear, or do, is for Him. For whatever good work we may do, let us not claim any praise or benefit. It is the Lord's; give up the fruits unto Him. Let us stand aside and think that we are only servants obeying the Lord, our Master, and that every impulse for action comes from Him every moment.*
> – *"Karma Yoga," The Complete Works of Swami Vivekananda*

If you believe in God, the path to non-attachment is more or less laid out for you. Whatever religion or belief system you choose to follow to deepen your belief in God, and/or achieve Oneness, has a long history and tradition for you to draw from. For example, in the Hindu tradition, we have three paths of yoga: Karma (works), Bhakti (devotion), and Jnana (knowledge). In Christianity, there are the sacraments and the practice of good works. Buddhism has the noble truths and the teachings of the Buddha. I personally don't know much about Judaism or Islam, but they are faiths I revere, and they have their own teachings on the path to Oneness with God.

I feel I would be doing you a disservice if I left you with ideas and tools that assumed your belief in God. Discerning how to achieve non-attachment without leaning on theism will be difficult, but I will try my best. My ruminations on this question of how to have non-attachment without a belief in God took me back, of all places, to junior varsity football.

In my 10th grade year, I met Coach Wilson. Coach Wilson was a first-year coach at our school and, at the time, was teaching in another school district. He was with us for practice, every day, and was one of the best coaches I've had throughout my time playing sports. It's worth mentioning, I was terrible at tackle football. Even though I took tons of physical punishment because I was slower, weaker, and smaller than most of the other kids on my team, and generally disliked the violence of football and the toxic culture of hyper-macho contact sports, it was worth playing just for the chance to learn this one thing from Coach Wilson: focus on playing (and practicing) your hardest, and the wins and losses will take care of themselves. Why? Once again, rather strangely, this line of inquiry took me to another seemingly random place: the Christian concept of faith—in the way I understand it as a non-baptized person, at least. What strikes me about religions I have studied is that each tradition has a goal that is fairly consistent: oneness with God. If you believe in God, what could be a better aspiration than to love God and be one with Him? Achieving this has variations, depending on the religion you are studying; each lays out different processes to follow. Christians have heaven, the Commandments, sacraments, profession of faith, direction to do good works, love, salvation, and grace through faith as promised in John 3:16, and the example of Jesus Himself to follow. Hindus have karma and guidance on how to break the cycle of rebirth, the teachings of the Vedas, Upanishads, and subsequent interpretations, like the paths of yoga that Swami Vivekananda lays out. Buddhists have nirvana and the teachings on how to get there.

These concepts, structures, and artifacts that lay out how to become one with God are a "process," one quite different from most other goals we set daily. Let's take health and professional goals as an example. We could set a goal of "I want to lose 10 pounds" or "I want to be certified as a practicing physician." Those goals are concrete. To some degree the goal of "oneness with God" is also concrete; it's a clear-cut goal because we have either achieved it or we have not, but unlike health and professional goals, it is NOT verifiable, there is no certificate or scale to prove it. Because losing ten pounds is verifiable, we try to verify it all the time by stepping on the scale. With such goals, the fact that we can easily verify them distracts us from doing the work to reach the goal itself. The easier goals are to verify, the more we focus on the measurement of the goal, rather than doing the actual work to achieve the verifiable change. By definition, we can't really know if we are one with God until after we've gone ahead. There is no scale we can step on to get an immediate answer. We will never fully know. Because it is non-verifiable, it's a bit easier to put the measurement of the goal out of our mind. If we can't know for sure whether we're going to be one with God after we die, we have no choice but to take a *leap of faith*. We can spend our time focused on the process our religious tradition has laid out for us; we can put in the work.

Let's go back to Coach Wilson, whose framework mirrors that of the non-verifiable goal of oneness with God: *focus on playing and practice your hardest* (i.e., putting work toward the process laid out in the religious tradition) *and the wins and losses will take care of themselves* (i.e., you will reach the non-verifiable goal of oneness with God).

In religious traditions, it becomes much easier to focus on the process when the goal ahead of the believer is non-verifiable. As believers, we focus on the process. There are stories, mythologies, scriptures, revelatory texts, interpretive texts, and music that provide lots of explanation, energy, and context on the beliefs, practices, and rituals for achieving oneness with God. So, what we have when we deconstruct the component parts of religious traditions (or Coach Wilson's lesson) are two things: the non-verifiable goal of oneness with God, and the process—the detailed, thoughtful, and compelling mythologies that explain the beliefs, rituals, and practices for how to reach that non-verifiable goal. When we lay it out this way, something is clearly missing, something characterized by a phrase stated at every Catholic mass we go to: "the mystery of faith." This mystery of faith, for our purposes, is similar to the concept of non-attachment. Think of it this way: you have a process laid out for you, that playing and practicing hard will help the team win games, maybe even a championship; but the thing is, that goal is not verifiable. Coach Wilson couldn't prove we would win a championship or even win more games than we lost. There was a logical leap to make between the process (playing and practicing hard) and the non-verifiable goal (winning games). In the example of religious tradition, we have this process laid out for us that everyone claims will bring us to oneness with God, but that goal is not verifiable. Nobody can actually prove that anyone has or has not achieved oneness with God. There is a logical leap to make between the process (the beliefs, rituals, and practices of the religious tradition) and the non-verifiable goal (oneness with God). Put another way, we must suspend the disbelief we have that the process will lead to the achievement of the goal. We have to ensure the process and the goal are not attached because that non-attachment frees us from constantly needing to verify the progress we are making. We must have faith.

Again, by having this sort of structure—a process and a non-verifiable goal—an act of faith (acceptance of the non-attachment between the process and the goal) emerges and is required. Faith is an act of non-attachment that emerges as a natural consequence of believing in the process and in the non-verifiable goal.

Now let's remember why we started talking about non-attachment in the first place: non-attachment helps us on our quest to be persistent by inoculating us from the desire to control the stories told about us, so we can stop making excuses that put us in our own way. Non-attachment is liberating. With faith, we can focus all our energy on the process itself.

Belief in God and committing to the processes prescribed by a religious tradition is one way to achieve non-attachment. Again, I don't want that to be *all* you have to lean on. Just because I am a theist doesn't allow me to assume you will be also. Even though you may not become a theist, the mental model around non-attachment that emerged after deconstructing Coach Wilson's lesson and the non-verifiable goal of oneness with God is useful. Having a non-verifiable goal, and a thoughtful, thorough process for achieving it, causes non-attachment to emerge as a natural consequence. Non-attachment becomes an externality rather than something we must blusteringly will ourselves to do, as Swami Vivekananda suggested.

I am not the first person to suggest that, committing ourselves to something much bigger than ourselves that we can't verify we've accomplished, is a path to peace and contentment. That is an old idea. David Brooks wrote a great book called *The Second Mountain: The Quest for a Moral Life*, which offers a simple, useful framework for thinking about how things beyond ourselves give us joy. Many people talk about how commitments to serving others turns out to be powerful. In a way, that is not surprising. Those types of commitments are non-verifiable; we are never "finished" with those goals. We can immerse ourselves in them and focus on the process instead of having anxiety over constantly verifying the outcome. There's a reason the loftiest, most non-verifiable goals liberate us: we can divert our attention from verification and the measurement of the result we seek, and focus on the process, on putting something positive out into the world. Non-verifiable goals force us to not attach. Having that same liberation and feeling of losing ourselves is much harder with verifiable goals because we "attach" to the act of verification so easily. Moreover, being thoughtful about the process matters. If the process is shallow, flawed, "too good to be true," or illogical, it's extremely hard to have faith in it! For non-verifiable goals, the process doesn't have shortcuts or an easy five-point checklist; in fact, we should be skeptical if the process seems easy or is too good to be true—not only because we know from experience that such snake oil rarely holds bud—but because having a rigorous process helps us to have non-attachment.

We should set non-verifiable goals, develop a process for achieving them, then immerse ourselves in the process. In a way, I suppose that's what I'm trying to write to you about in these letters. My non-verifiable goal is to become a good man who continuously chooses goodness over power, so I can fulfill my duty as a father to help you become a good person. The process involves the beliefs, rituals, and practices that underlie the three cornerstone virtues: curiosity; courage; and persistence. My hope is that, by convincing us that the non-verifiable goal (goodness) is worthwhile, and that the process (curiosity, courage, and persistence) is rigorous and effective, we'll take a leap of faith, choose the work, and walk the path of goodness.

A lot has changed in the past five years. You have each grown up so much since you've entered this world. Emmett is babbling and sitting up. Myles is running, talking, and moving with daring energy into everything he does. Bo is thinking, feeling, and starting to do bona fide mathematics. Before you three were born, I used to run, watch TV, and even be hungover (too much) on the weekends. Now, I get up early with you boys while mommy gets a little extra sleep. We just hang out. We laugh, we sing, we play with Dinos on the floor or play Uno (with mommy, sometimes, too). We dance and we cook breakfast together. So much has changed and I didn't think I could have so much everyday joy in my life.

I am so grateful for you, Robert, Myles, and Emmett. Thank you for making it so that, as I took this leap of faith, I was blessed with so much joy because of it. I hope I can give back more joy to you than you have already given to me.

Love,
Your Papa

* * *

16

Time

**To think so long into the future,
without going crazy, one must be an optimist.**

May 20, 2019

My Sons,

At the time I first wrote this letter, your mother, Robert, and I were on a trip to England. Mimi, Granddad, and Uncle B came too, but they have continued ahead to Windsor. The three of us (and Myles, then unborn) were spending time with your Great Aunt Tricia and her family in Norfolk.

Robert, you were having a wonderful nap on a beautiful day. Mommy had just gone up to join you. Auntie Tricia and I were just having a wonderful chat that has inspired me to write while we have some downtime.

We have just left our dialogue on persistence, about non-attachment, and how leaps of faith emerge after we connect rigorous processes with a non-verifiable goal. The question you are probably asking then is: *How do we develop a rigorous process and conceptualize a non-verifiable goal?* I have been thinking about this. I have been focused, for weeks now, on time.

What is beautiful about non-verifiable goals is how we, by definition, can't verify if we've achieved the goal. If we can manage to articulate a non-verifiable goal, it's a gift that takes pressure, self-editing, fear of judgment and, in turn, excuses, out of the picture. The inability to verify the goal sets us free.

Part of what makes a non-verifiable goal non-verifiable is time and how we contemplate it. When we have a verifiable goal, it must be measurable within our lifetime. It's easy to see that non-verifiable goals are more primed to have long or indefinite timescales. To get the freedom we seek from a non-verifiable goal, it *must* be on an indefinite timescale so we don't even try to verify the goal. If a goal can be achieved in the short run, even if it is technically non-verifiable, we'll want to verify it. We would be measuring ourselves all the time. Let's say I want to make the best pancake that has ever been made. That's surely a non-verifiable goal because I cannot try any of the delicious pancakes made in the past. However, I can make pancakes quickly, right now. When I make that batch, I can ask you and others to try them immediately. I can ask if it is the best pancake you and they have ever had. And yes, I could never actually verify if that pancake is the best one ever made in history, but because I can make that pancake right now, I can easily fool myself into trying to verify, at least to some degree, this non-verifiable goal. When I try to verify that non-verifiable goal, I will easily get caught in the cycle of self-editing, judgment, fear, and excuses because I will be so worried about what everyone thinks about my pancakes.

The only way to ensure a goal is non-verifiable, with

certainty, is to have the time horizon for the goal extend beyond our own life. Because of this, we must be able to think in long, and sometimes *indefinitely long*, time horizons to set them, and we need to do this consistently, in real life settings. If the non-attachment that non-verifiable goals help us to achieve is a cornerstone of persistence, thinking along indefinitely long-time scales is an unavoidable skill for us to develop. If we do not, it will become extremely difficult, in practice, to articulate and pursue a non-verifiable goal that helps us get out of the cycle of excuses that thwart our persistence.

This intuition about thinking in longer time horizons and time horizons beyond our own lives is not a new idea. In business books and lectures, it has become common to hear pundits talking about how important it is for "leaders to think long term." But what is usually frustratingly missing, in my experience, is any concrete thought on how to do that. Let's think of something you are most likely to be the world expert on: your life. Think about your life and what you hope it will be like in 25, even 10 years from now. It's a hard question, right? We don't know how we, or the world, will change in even five or seven years, let alone 10 or 25 years. For a non-verifiable goal, we might have to think 50, 100, or 150 years into the future, the equivalent of asking about what your great-great-grandchildren's or great-, great-, great-, great-, great grandchildren's world might be like, which is simply mind-bending.

I see you, Robert, interact with your great-grandparents— your lives are worlds apart. Your nana and great Granddad were just telling us a few days ago, when we were staying with them, that they grew up using outdoor toilets. They were born less than 90 years before you, a relatively modest range when thinking about setting non-verifiable goals. Now imagine the world you were born into in 2017, which was so different than the time they were growing up.

One deep lens that affects timescales is gratitude. Let's consider the likely mindset of someone who thinks in short-term timescales and someone who thinks in indefinite, long-time scales. The short-term thinker doesn't think past the next year, month, or maybe even tomorrow. This is the person who wants to get whatever they want right now, the one who doesn't invest for the future, the person who lives hedonistically today because tomorrow may not come. When I suggest the mindset of a short-term thinker, I'm talking about the person who doesn't feel efficacy for future generations because they've been burned and isolated and, consequently, has no empathy for those coming up behind them. These people exist, and though I have described them harshly, they may not have bad intentions. I've heard about such young men and women from people close to us—either from friends of our family who taught middle and high school in the city, or from colleagues at the Detroit Police Department who work with youth on gun and gang violence prevention. They have shared how these young folks are traumatized or struggling and, as a result, don't think more than a few hours ahead into the future because they don't know if they will be alive that long. It's the sort of mentality you'd only expect to find if you were in a war zone. I vividly remember a conversation I had with the lead of the department's Gang Intelligence Unit who described how some young men in Detroit live with the fear that they might get shot *anywhere at any time,* and literally must live hour by hour. When I started hearing these observations from others—teachers, police officers, clergy, community activists, and basketball coaches—it was jarring.

In addition to the metaphor of short-term thinkers often having a "war zone" mentality, a gentler word that comes to mind is pessimism. People who think really short-term are often pessimistic about the future, either because they are uncertain about it or think it will be bad; or worse, think they won't be around.

I've found that people who think on longer time scales are optimistic about the future. To think so long into the future, without going crazy, one must be an optimist. It's far too depressing to think about the future unless there's hope for something good ahead. In effect, if you think about the future and change your actions in the short term, even to some degree, you must believe the future is possible and worth thinking about. You need to believe you do not need to rush and enjoy hedonic pleasures, or simply just survive in the short term because something better, deeper, or sweeter is out there in the future. If you thought about the future, and didn't have optimism, you'd spiral into a cycle of woe and worry. Thinking about the future from a posture of pessimism is destructive, draining. If we want to be constructive when we think about the future, we should embrace reality, but it also behooves us to be optimists rather than pessimists. Being an optimist, at a minimum, makes it easier to get through the daily grind. These observations are theory, though grounded in many years of experience observing people; however, being an optimist may not be sufficient to help us think long term. To think on a long-time scale, particularly one that surpasses our own lifetime, optimism isn't enough. Optimism may make thinking about the future more tolerable, but there's no reason to think it can reliably help us think beyond the timescale of our own lives. We need a strong conviction to help us, to free us to imagine what we will not experience.

I think we need to believe there is something transcendent, bigger than our own lives. How can we think beyond our own lives if we don't believe there is anything of value that goes beyond our lives, something that could possibly transcend us? We must believe such a thing exists, that there is something bigger and more beautiful than our individual life, something transcendently beautiful, virtuous, significant, enduring, intangible. Something we know is special and worth contributing to. Friendship is transcendent. Art and music are transcendent. The creation of knowledge and the deepening of faith are transcendent. Nature and the cosmos can be transcendent. The human body is transcendent. Sincerity, honesty, love, and commitment are transcendent.

If we believe there's nothing sufficiently beautiful to transcend, why would we think beyond our bodies and lives? What would be the point?

Let me recap the logical claim we have going here: if we want to be persistent, we must not get in our own way with excuses. One way to not make excuses is to practice non-attachment. One important way to develop the capability to not be attached is to pursue a non-verifiable goal. To even contemplate a non-verifiable goal, we need to think and operate on an indefinitely long-time scale that extends beyond our own lives. The ability to think and operate on an indefinitely long-time scale requires something stronger than optimism: it requires an appreciation of transcendent beauty, somewhere beyond just us. This leads us to a simple question: How does one develop an appreciation for some transcendently beautiful thing?   One way to develop this appreciation is to look for diamonds, those infinite exquisite things: a beautiful music composition; a masterful work of art; stars as they appear in a remote location unpolluted by city lights—all things worth protecting, observing, and preserving.

What makes these diamonds special, but also impractical, is that we don't experience them every day. Even though we in Detroit have access to incredible collections of art at the Detroit Institute of Arts, we can't practically visit the DIA every day. And for every one diamond we come across, there are many more patches of rough. So, what we can do is find beauty in the rough. If we can find something transcendent in the grind and muck of day-to-day life, we can have constant reminders that there are beautiful, wonderful things beyond us, rather than going long durations and through great trouble to have these moments of transcendent awe. If most of our life is mundane and typical or has some level of sadness or struggle, we need to try to find beauty in the daily grind, which makes up most of the days we have on this earth.

The best way I know to find beauty in the rough is to practice gratitude. When we force ourselves to express gratitude, even in the most boring or difficult moments, we are forced to look for beautiful things around us, which may be hidden in plain sight. If I committed, let's say, to expressing three things I'm grateful for today, either in writing or vocally, I am committing to the process of looking for something of beauty in everyday life, wherever I can find it. Gratitude could then also be called "the practice of finding the beauty in what's around us, on purpose."

That's what I try to do every day: find three things I am grateful for. Even on the roughest day. Either writing in my journal, whispering them in prayer, or saying them out loud to someone else, usually your mother, who first exposed me to the beauty of practicing gratitude, one of the most beautiful gifts I have ever received. The more I practice gratitude, the easier it is to find beauty. Gratitude cleans our usually dusty lenses with which we view the world. The more we practice, the cleaner and more focused that lens becomes.

I fear all I am saying to you seems robotic and rigid, as if the pursuit of persistence or goodness is a militaristic march toward some sort of idealized nirvana. Or that humility and gratitude are a practice you need to "win at," that the virtues at its foundation—curiosity, courage, and persistence—are some sort of game to be won or something to be conquered. They are not. The daily practice of gratitude or humility is a good reminder of this. Gratitude and humility are practices that ultimately have a huge effect on the development of your character. They inject an ethos in us that helps us remember that the world and life itself don't exist solely to serve and elevate us. They shift our thinking from ourselves, our own needs, and turn our gaze to the needs of others and the broader world. The infinite wisdom of gratitude and humility is that there is so much in this life outside of us. There is so much beauty outside of us. There are so many things that transcend us. Cerebral connections to perceptions of time and persistence, and gratitude and humility, are so important on a gut level. I found, once I started practicing gratitude, that it opened my heart. It made me kinder and released my anger. That wasn't precisely my intent, but it did. It made me appreciate and love others more deeply. It has helped me to let little things go and forgive more quickly. Gratitude and humility, and committing to their practice, has made me a better man, the sort of man I think I want to be and the man I have said I wanted to be.

I have two more topics to write to you about related to persistence, but I think this is a good point in our journey to rush to the punch line of what this is all for because the whole point of sharing these ideas and these letters with you is not to have some sort of cerebral, academic exercise. The point is for us to be better men, able to choose goodness over power, and to do so consistently.

What does that really mean? That's what I hope to share with you now, and I'm excited. What I will write in my next letter has slowly been connecting in my head for over a year now. I hope it ends up being helpful to you.

Love,
Your Papa

* * *

17

Sacrifice

Trying to live up to the principles of telling the truth, loving unconditionally, and making sacrifices are good rules of thumb to get us through.

July 2, 2019

My Sons,

I have written these letters to you for over two years for a fairly straightforward purpose. It is my mission and responsibility to help you become good people. The best ways I thought of to do that are to try to become a better person myself, being present in your life, and letting my actions speak louder than my words. In my first letter to you, my challenge quickly became trying to figure out, from first principles, how to make myself a better man and, more importantly, figure out why doing something so hard was important in the first place. What I came to understand in my reflections is the importance of choices. Choices, after all, are where thoughts and actions are revealed, laid bare, and made real in the world. As I have told you, the most difficult tradeoff to make is between goodness and power. When I say, "choosing the work" or "walk the path of goodness," I mean choosing goodness. I mean that when making a choice that has a tradeoff between goodness and power, to choose the option that reflects goodness, even though choosing power may feel more comfortable, palatable, or intoxicating. To choose goodness means to navigate the tradeoff between goodness and power consistently as we make hundreds, maybe thousands of choices a day.

We are up north as I'm writing this for our annual holiday (Bo just woke up from a nap and we are about to have lunch before a boat ride) and today we had pasties for lunch. I had a choice between having hot sauce, BBQ sauce, or no sauce with my lunch. That choice has little moral consequence, at least today. It's a preference between roughly equivalent, benign options. Many choices are similar. They aren't a tradeoff between goodness and power. Some choices don't have high stakes, morally speaking. Other choices are the inverse. They can have extremely high stakes morally, financially, emotionally, or otherwise. These sorts of choices affect the course of your life and the lives of the people you love—what your granddad calls inflection points. The greatest of these inflection points is who you marry, but also where you live, big moves in your professional life, or a tragic loss. These are the big decisions which require data, logic, analysis, and soul searching. These are decisions where you must counter the effects of cognitive biases by defining principles and criteria up front that you can lean on. Though these inflection points are colossally important, they don't happen often; they are one-in-a-million moments that are a big deal when they *do* happen.

Most decisions we make in a day have moral and social effects, but none of them will change the course of our lives on their own. The thing is, in a day, we make a mess load of these independently inconsequential but collectively damning decisions. Every individual decision feels innocuous, like the way we choose to greet someone in the morning. Or whether we choose to stay up an extra hour watching television. Or what we choose to read, buy, or share with others about ourselves. It's whether we choose to make little sacrifices, like sharing our cookies with a friend, or the parties we choose to attend. It's something small, like how we conduct ourselves in a meeting at work or whether we tell a white lie or not. It's the decision about whether we choose to share our feelings or to be sarcastic toward our family. Even what we choose to think about while daydreaming or riding the subway. These decisions, though individually consequential, are collectively damning because we make so many of them over the course of our daily lives. They compound. If we choose to never smile at strangers we pass on the sidewalk, it compounds. If we choose to stay up an extra hour every night for a decade, it compounds. If we choose to read trashy tabloids or sensational websites, it compounds. If we think about how great we are and how everyone else is lesser than us, while we're driving to work every day, it compounds. These "little" decisions are not merely tiny details that make up the footnotes in our lives. Because we are the choices we make, these aggregated "little" decisions come to define who we are and our character. These are the decisions of mine, which will most influence your character. Whether or not you learn goodness from me by example will depend on my small choices that really aren't small at all.

So, there is an important lesson for me here. I need to try my best to be a good person in these "little" moments. Don't get me wrong—the decisions we make at inflection points matter, but they happen so infrequently that, if I walk the path of goodness at the inflection points but choose power at all the rest, my life will end up bending toward the pursuit of power.

How we make little decisions shapes how we make big decisions anyway. Little decisions compound to shape our character *and* how we choose to act, carrying over to how we act when we're at an inflection point.

There are so many not-actually-little decisions, we can't apply a rigorous, analytical, data-driven decision-making process to all of them. If we did, we wouldn't be able to function in the real world. We would spend our whole lives in analysis paralysis. Our capacity to make intentional, conscious, analytically rigorous decisions is limited. After a while, we get decision fatigue or just run out of daylight. We need shortcuts. We need to make many of our decisions on autopilot. There is no other way to function in our daily lives if we don't use heuristics to make a lot of decisions. What this means is that we make most decisions without really thinking about them—from *muscle memory*!

To persist in any endeavor, we need the right muscle memory to push us toward what we want to do and the sort of people we want to become. To walk the path of goodness, for example, we can't face every decision with paralysis and doubt. We have to act. We have to move forward. So, it's critical to have the heuristics, that muscle memory, for how we live our daily lives. The conviction I have is that if we are committed to this practice of character development, of choosing the work, we can develop muscle memory that leads us to choose goodness over power. That's essentially what these letters have been an exercise for: developing muscle memory that leads to goodness.

Now, my sons, I owe you an answer to questions I hope you have been wondering about: What does it look like to be a good person? What does a good person, when they have developed the muscle memory to choose goodness over power, actually do? Though there's thousands of years of work in moral philosophy—from Aristotle, Kant, Mill, Singer, Scanlon—our lives are real; they are not thought experiments, moral dilemmas, or trolley problems. These are our lives, my sons. These are *your lives.* Over these past few years, I've tried to think about what someone who walks the path of goodness consistently does, in real life. What are the heuristics, the muscle memories, good people have? Here are the heuristics I keep coming back to: tell the truth; love unconditionally; and make sacrifices. They are probably not the only heuristics that matter, but they are the best three I have come up with so far.

Let me tell you where these ideas come from. As I have become a father, I have learned, over and over again, how Dada has shaped the person and parent I have become. I always thought I was influenced the most by the great men and women of history and literature, like Gandhi, Socrates, and Atticus Finch, even Hermione Granger—just to name a few. How foolish a thought that was! My papa has affected my life more than anyone. He may not be a man history will remember, but he was an uncommon man of the most unshakable integrity and the strongest devotion. He was so humble and unassuming, I would say, that only a few people knew how great of a man he was. My papa, your dada, had the muscle memory for goodness. One of my most haunting regrets in life is that I didn't fully appreciate the man he was when I was growing up, nor did I realize my mistake soon enough to be able to tell him how much I respect and admire him before he went ahead.

I don't remember a time when telling the truth wasn't impressed upon me. Your Dada (and Dadi) drilled it into my head. It was not negotiable or something they had to convince me of. It was simply expected of me. And I expect the same from you three. Every branch of our family—on my side, on your mother's side—tells the truth. It's just what we do. Everyone that matters to us, that we let into our world, including friends, tells the truth. We simply don't keep the company of liars.

Telling the truth is valuable beyond our own character development. It's a powerful rule for daily life because it's a gracious act. Big lies are one thing, but people often get caught when telling them. People get away with smaller lies all the time. Lying has big costs to the community because even a few liars destroy that community's bond. If you know there are liars around, how can you trust anyone? And if you don't have trust in the community, everything is harder, darker, and more costly. When someone lies, the whole community loses.

I never spent much time with my maternal grandparents (or paternal for that matter) because, unfortunately, India is so far away and, when I was growing up, we could never afford yearly trips to go visit them. But your Dadi told me stories of her parents, your great grandparents, Nana and Nani. Of all the stories I heard, those that always stuck out to me were the ones about how they treated people who were not their family by blood. You'll have to ask Dadi about the details, but she would always tell me about how children from their neighborhood would come over and Nani would feed them and take care of them just like they were her own biological children. Dadi told me about how Nana would fund the education of other children, without making a big deal about it and without asking for anything in return. From the stories I heard, it seems as if it was natural and expected for there to always be someone from outside my mom's gaggle of siblings under the charge of my grandparents. I didn't realize it at the time, but just hearing those stories gave me a lens for understanding every act of unconditional love and every unconditional community commitment I've witnessed since. It never dawned on me that you could love and care for someone else so effortlessly and sincerely, especially people you aren't related to. But you can. You can love someone without any conditions, qualifications, or prejudices—that's unconditional love. This is all the more remarkable because loving someone is hard to begin with. It's much easier to be hurt the closer you are to them. By loving them, you put yourself in a position, on purpose, to be hurt. You have no recourse, all your cards are on the table, yet people love unconditionally anyway. And what is love, really, if it's not unconditional? Unconditional love is magical. It brings people out of dark places. It is the foundational gift that seeds the creation of communities: in church congregations or in regional hubs of entrepreneurship where the older generation mentors the new. It is what raises self-assured, generous children. It is the fertilizer that causes culture to grow. Unconditional love gives life and is selfless and gracious.

Unconditional love and telling the truth are manifestations of the same general idea: sacrifice. Again, sacrifice is when someone (likely consciously) compares their needs to those of another, then chooses to forego their needs to meet those of the other. Consider what an act of grace and generosity a sacrifice is! First, I must understand what I want and need. Then, I'm going to take the time to understand your wants and needs. Then, I'm going to be honest and self-aware enough to admit that my needs conflict with yours. When I realize this, I don't try to ignore what I've realized. On top of all the emotional labor I have already done, I'm going to give up what I want and need so you can have what you want and need and I'm not going to make you pay me back for it later. And peculiarly, after I sacrifice for you, I feel happiness, perhaps even joy. What a remarkable and special thing it is to sacrifice. Sacrifice is one of the heuristics good people tend to have, it's part of their muscle memory—in my observation at least.

I should tell you that I have come to this observation and conclusion about sacrifice (and honesty and love, for that matter) secularly. Even though I think I mostly came to this thought about sacrifice that way, informed by my own life experiences, I was surely influenced by the two religious traditions that run deeply in our family: Hinduism and Christianity. In the Hindu tradition, we have the four main paths to God—the yogas—one of which is *karma yoga*. The deep lesson here is that a path to God through karma (action) is about works. Karma yoga is about being able to do works and deeds dutifully, and for their own sakes, not because of the reward they present us. Sound familiar? It's sacrifice. I am not a scholar of Christianity, but I'm also reminded of a scene from the New Testament that was shared in a homily at mass in the past year. Jesus is in the Garden of Gethsemane after the last supper. He knows he will be crucified the next day. He goes into the garden and is in agony, sweating blood. Yet, he does not flee. He stays his course, is crucified the next morning, and rises three days after. According to Christian theology, because Jesus went forward with this, the sins of man were forgiven, and we have the chance to have oneness with our Father who art in heaven. Love and pain for others' sake. Sound familiar? It's sacrifice.

It is a good heuristic for day-to-day decisions to question ourselves when a sacrifice presents itself. Rather than justifying to ourselves why we *should* make a sacrifice, maybe it's more in line with the virtue of goodness to assume we should make a sacrifice and justify why we *shouldn't*.

I admit that these three gracious acts: telling the truth; unconditional love; and sacrifice, more generally, may not be complete or perfect heuristics. But they are something strong to weave into our muscle memory as we navigate daily life, so we do not have to analytically reason out every decision of moral consequence we ever encounter. Trying to live up to the principles of telling the truth, loving unconditionally, and making sacrifices are good rules of thumb to get us through. Trying to make these gracious acts are what our journey is for. They are ends in themselves. That's what this is all for, my sons. If we can live persistently with truth, love, and sacrifice, we will have done our duty. That's what we are persisting to do, over and over. Truth, love, and sacrifice are what walking the path of goodness—in real life—is all about.

Love,
Your Papa

* * *

18

Don't Beat Yourself

**Without hope, a mortal man has no desire or energy to
change his nature.**

July 15, 2019

My Sons,

Before we return to one last session of reflection, I figured
you may all appreciate some practical tips. At the time I am
writing this, we just spent a wonderful weekend together as a
family and watched the Wimbledon final. Of note was a 5-set
gentlemen's final, where Roger Federer and Novak Djokovic
had three tiebreaks in the match, including the first ever fifth
set tiebreak after the set score reached 12-12. It was incredible
to watch.

A sure way to lose a tennis match is to beat yourself. You
beat yourself by hitting the ball into the net, hitting it wildly
out of bounds, or double faulting on a serve. As mentioned
before, these shots are "unforced errors." If you minimize
unforced errors, even against a tough opponent, you have a

pretty decent chance of winning a tennis match. The same thinking can apply to choices you make, and to persistence. If you avoid unforced errors, you can put yourself in a good position to walk the path of goodness and avoid the temptation of power.

If you choose to marry, who you choose to marry will be the biggest decision of your life. If you marry the right person, everything in your life falls much more into place. Your granddad talks about this all the time. Marrying the right person is like being a sea captain who always has fair winds— it just makes everything smoother and easier. The big question is how to know who the right person is. That's an important question, I suppose, but I don't know that it's the first one I'd ask. My first question would be whether *you* are prepared, ready, mature enough, and interested enough to marry *anyone*. Because once you know in your heart you are ready to be a married person, you can consider whether the person in front of you is the right person. For discussion's sake, let's say you are ready. Then what? When people say, "when you know, you know," I think that's true, but it's not that helpful. I would describe "when you know, you know" as a representation of a shift in mindset.

A pros-and-cons list is the most commonly used tool for making decisions I have ever come across. Your mother loves them. Related to these lists are checklists or scoring rubrics which use pre-defined criteria to help make less-biased decisions. Pros-and-cons lists are terrific, especially for decisions like buying a car or house or choosing whether to take a new job, because they help identify whether your preferences are aligned with the option in front of you or not. When choosing who to marry, I've found that alignment of preferences isn't the goal. When you are marrying someone, you're literally vowing to make sacrifices for your partner in sickness, health, wealth, and poverty. Aligned preferences don't get you through hard times, exactly. What you're really trying to figure out is whether you are prepared for, and perhaps even looking forward to, making sacrifices for the person you are marrying. For me, that was the big turning point in my mindset. When I realized I wasn't trying to understand whether I would like how your mom would make me feel as my wife but, rather, I felt acceptance and perhaps even gratitude for the chance to sacrifice things I wanted in order to build a life with her and elevate her, I knew. When you know, you know. Being married is hard, even to your mother who is a really easy person to be married to because of how loving, fun, smart, and strong she is. I thank God every day that I get to be married to your mother. As we've been together and married longer, your mother has changed my life.

I swear I'm not trying to be funny by saying this, but one of the biggest ways she has changed my life is with sleep and rest. Your mother loves sleep. Epically. Which is great because a sure-fire way to beat yourself is to not sleep and rest enough. Before I met your mother, I didn't care much about sleep. I stayed up late and woke up early. I had always been like that. It's not that I avoided sleep, I just liked being awake better. Turned out, that was an exhausting way to live. I didn't realize how tired I was until I actually started sleeping. Now I try hard to get 7-8 hours, even though when you all were newborns that was tough. There are so many studies about sleep, and interest in sleep has only been growing as I have aged. If the science doesn't convince you to sleep, God help you. You, meaning you specifically, Bo, make bad decisions when you're tired and are particularly cranky, too. Even when you were first learning to walk. When you're tired, you bump into tables and scream a lot. Myles and Emmett, you were the same way. Seriously though, it's hard to control impulses and anger when we're sleepy, and that matters a lot. If you get my point and need no convincing, great. If you don't get it, it's probably not an error in judgment. Like me, you probably believe you have too much to do, or somehow haven't earned the right to sleep and rest. You have. You have earned that right. But honestly, there's nothing you need to earn. You don't need anyone's approval or permission to get a decent night's sleep. Besides, your work will surely be worthless anyway if you're not rested. There are certainly times when you will want to or can't help but sacrifice sleep, but if you make sleep a priority and a habit, you can sneak in a few nights here and there where you stay up late without being too worse for the wear.

Seriously. Get your sleep. Not being well rested is an unforced error.

There are many easy unforced errors I am not an expert on, but I will list some of them here, and you can read about them on your own and decide whether or not my advice is worth following.

DON'T EAT GARBAGE. If you stick to fresh foods—mostly plants, and unfried—and modest portions, you'll stay fairly healthy. Think of food as medicine or poison. If you eat well, you won't have to spend major time, energy, or money managing chronic health issues. Eating poorly is an unforced error.

EXERCISE. This makes you feel good and is fun. If you stay healthy, you will have the mental and physical energy to focus on other things. Being a couch potato is an unforced error.

GETTING HIGH, DRUNK, ETC. I'd admit, I enjoy an occasional drink—"papa juice," as we call it around the house nowadays. But after many mistakes (and hangovers), I try to avoid being drunk or even tipsy anymore. I am dramatically more likely to make a horrible decision or waste a day when I'm drunk. Also, drugs and alcohol weaken your ability to deal with problems by sheltering you from tough emotions. Being wasted is an unforced error.

LIVE BELOW YOUR MEANS. Your mother and I don't live lavishly for a reason. Being short of money is terrible. It is all-consuming and a huge source of stress with effects that sometimes linger for years. If you live below your means, you can dramatically reduce your risk and your stress. It's still possible to live a good life and have lots of fun (it's not hard, especially in a city as great as ours) to find leisure without spending much money. It's really hard to live paycheck to paycheck, but it doesn't take hundreds of thousands of dollars a year (in today's dollars) to live a meaningful life. If you think it does, you're looking in the wrong places or missing the beauty and joy hidden in plain sight. Outspending your wallet is an unforced error.

EXPRESS YOURSELF. When I was growing up, it was said—even joked about on television shows—that men don't express their feelings. Dopey male characters were portrayed as being incapable of doing it. But honestly, it is hard for everyone, not just men. Just do it. Just try. It can be as simple as completing the sentence, "I feel...," in a journal. Or you can express yourself in other ways, like art, music, dance, building something with your hands, cooking, and so many more ways. Express yourself even when it feels uncomfortable or unnatural. Keeping your feelings locked up, only to explode later, is an unforced error.

LET LOVE IN. The world can feel like a scary place and people can seem untrustworthy, even people close to you. Let them love you. Let them care about you. Become interdependent. Loneliness can come from not loving others, but it more often comes from not letting them love you. What's the point of all this if you are closed out from the world? Closing your heart to others is an unforced error and a crushing way to live.

Those are some of the most obvious unforced errors to me, but there are surely more.

—

Now, I don't for a moment believe that simply trying to avoid unforced errors is a key to life. I have not found that merely avoiding mistakes leads to a life of happiness, joy, goodness, or anything that great. To heed my advice and avoid those unforced errors is a way to subsist and is perhaps good guidance on how to prevent catastrophically bad outcomes.

But why not just subsist? Why not just do the basics, go through the motions, and avoid unforced errors? You'd be a pretty good person. You can probably have a comfortable life, especially if you pick a well-paying profession and work decently hard. Why not just do that? I can attest to you that this is not a trivial matter. There are times in my life I did not have a lot of hope. One of those times was in my early twenties just before I met your mother. As I told you many pages ago, those were dark times. In those days, I wondered if I should just lower my expectations, do the basics, and go along for the ride. For a while, maybe I did. In those days, I suppose I had a lot of fun just being single in the city, making friends, pretending to be cool, I guess. But despite the fun, I still had little hope that the life I really wanted—something like the life your mother and I have started to build together—was possible. Without hope, a mortal man has no desire or energy to change his nature. To have no hope is to be shackled to a life. If you go through the motions and avoid unforced errors, life can be decent enough, but I suppose it's not really a full life. It's something to be done on autopilot, biding time until you reach a final destination. Without hope, that is what we can expect.

But hope is a feeling that an important dream, our *most important* dream, is still possible. With hope, even in the slightest most unlikely way, that dream is still possible. Like we talked about with processes and non-verifiable goals, to have hope, we must have a dream we deeply believe in, but also a plan we trust can get us there. Luckily, your mother is exceptionally good at so many aspects of planning, ones I am grateful she has taught me. She takes big challenges and breaks them down into smaller categories of tasks. She puts them on timelines. She creates organized, simple systems for tracking progress and staying on time. She is skilled at delivering priorities and planning the order of operations. That is why we have great weekends together and fun, relatively stress-free vacations. Everything you need to know about planning and execution and making your dreams achievable you can learn from her. And if you read some books, you'll be a master in no time.

Knowing I would be finishing this letter to you this evening, I asked your mother for some additional advice, the sort of wisdom earned from experience, something you can't find in a book: "What separates a truly great plan that is created by a master from a plan created by an average person?" First, she reiterated the essence of planning: start with your end goal—the dream, if you will, and work backwards to find the straightest path. To get from point A to point B, you must define A and B, then put the journey between on a timeline. This is much easier said than done and is truly wise. All great plans begin with the end in mind. But then your mother said something truly remarkable that I would have never thought of on my own: *that what really separates an exceptional plan from one that is merely average is adjustments.* Great plans require adjustments because no plan ever actually goes to plan. A modestly good planner compares how the plan is going to reach the desired end goal and makes adjustments, but holds firm to the components of the plan that aren't supposed to change. This is counterintuitive, but brilliant. Exceptional planners are those who know when to change the plan, sometimes boldly. The lesson here, in relation to persistence, is simple: to persist, we must adjust. So, an exceptional plan requires two things: a clear, compelling end goal and effective adjustments. Imagining and envisioning a dream is difficult, and it is not always obvious how to do that. It's not always easy to make adjustments to a plan. Luckily, these challenges are special cases of a broader activity I happen to be pretty good at: reflection. In fact, other than making pancakes, reflection might be the only other thing in the world I'm truly excellent at!

So that's where we will end this very long and special journey that we mortal men have embarked on: a quick discussion on reflection. I have always planned to write another volume focused on reflection and I have already started drafting it.

What I have realized over the past few pages is that maybe I've written these letters to you backwards. Or at least a bit out of order. Where we started was with the question of *why goodness?* But, in a way, that question is inextricably linked with the question we touched on today: Why do anything more than go through the motions? The answer, of course, is the hope that our dreams might be possible. The discussion of "why goodness," in a way, presupposes that we must have hope and that we do have hope—for something—at all. That we have dreams at all. That we are capable of even understanding the soul within us enough to have hopes and dreams. Only then does it matter if we have the curiosity, courage, and persistence to act to make those hopes and dreams the truth of our lives. If we don't have hope, and we're just going to go through the motions, why bother with curiosity, courage, and persistence? Why bother with goodness? These letters to you, then, have been a quest for hope or at least some articulation of my dreams and plans as a father to you three, my children, my sons. It is my dream as your father to love you unconditionally and raise you to be good people.

Through writing these letters to you, I had hoped to think about how I might do that. When I realized the best way to raise you to be good people was to become a better man myself, I explored the question of how to become a good person, on purpose, as deeply as I could. Now, I have a plan with three components: be curious; be courageous; and be persistent. When I wrote my first letters to you, months before Bo was born, I was uncertain whether I could be the father you all needed me to be. Now I have hope.

And so, these letters are coming to a close, but we must discuss reflection, which is really what started this quest for me, for had I not even reflected on fatherhood and the dreams I had for myself and for your mother and me together, or for the dreams I had for you as my sons, I would have never picked up a pen.

So, my sons, let's go. Let us meditate on reflection and take rest. It is a fitting end, which, in many ways, was the beginning of it all.

Love,
Papa

* * *

19

Opening My Eyes

Will we try to be better, or will we refuse?
What, my sons, will you choose?

August 17, 2019

My Three Sons,

I distinctly remember when I started writing this collection of letters. We were visiting your granddad's family in Europe for your Aunt Ellie's wedding. I had just purchased a black Moleskine notebook from a store in the airport in Nice, France, on a whim no less, with a few minutes to spare before boarding started. Your mother (and Robert, because he was in the womb) was sleeping in the seat next to me on the modestly sized plane. I started writing. Two and a half years later, I am wrapping up.

I already know I will write more on how to reflect at some point, but as I alluded to you in my last letter, it took me hundreds of pages and thousands of words to realize that the reason I even started thinking and writing to you about goodness was because of the process of reflection. Reflecting is what started all this. So perhaps it is fitting that this last letter to you is about reflection itself. It is and has always been something critical to any worthwhile pursuits I have attempted.

A lot has changed in the two plus years that have passed since the first letter I wrote on the plane from Nice to London. Most notably and importantly, you three are here. What has changed, most deeply, is what we are. We are a family. What we focus on is family. *Family first* is axiom #1 for your mom and me. This, perhaps, has always been the case for your mother, but for me, this is new in a way.

Before I met your mother, I talked about family being important, but it was not always reflected in my actions. From the outside, it would have been easy to see that family may have mattered, even greatly, but it was not *first*. My time, money, and energy were obviously and ridiculously spent on myself—mostly on my "career" and the sort of hedonistic experiences and luxuries a bachelor in a city, being paid more than he deserves, indulges in. My focus was on myself, not on others. Family was a sideshow; my professional life was the main event.

But we've made adjustments, your mother and I. And I am grateful for, and proud of, the adjustments we have made because our actions—my actions, specifically—are now focused on family. We spend most Sundays with family. We talk to your grandparents nearly every day. Your mother and I continue our weekly temperature check and rarely miss it, to this day. I changed my job, mostly because it was making it difficult to be a husband and a father, even though working in public service was what I loved and felt called to do. We don't use cell phones at the dinner table, ever, anymore, and we talk about how we are really doing, instead of just exchanging pleasantries. I do not bring this up to boast in any way; I share it because I want to pick apart why we made those adjustments; they didn't happen spontaneously—they took intention and work.

We are mortal men. We are not born perfect and perhaps we are not even born that great. We can't know for sure, but we certainly can't assume we're perfect beings, so we must adjust—learning and growing as we get older and taller—and hopefully become better people.

In this craft and practice of becoming a better man, it is not as simple as taking a class, reading a philosophy book, or getting some sort of certificate like it can be for other skills we learn, like driving a car or managing other people's money. Those activities are surface-level even if they are important. Becoming a better man is an extremely important pursuit, but it's not something that's easily explained or learned. It's a deep change that's hard, and there's no real guidebook of wisdom to draw from.

To become a better man, it takes adjusting to so many things: our bodies; minds; beliefs; behaviors; practices; and more. The deep change to become a better man requires improving upon everything but our soul, which is immaterial and unchangeable. We must improve upon everything but the Atman.

I know of only one way that this deep change—improving upon everything but the soul—starts. The first step of deep change is reflection, the honest introspective kind. To reflect is hard, but not complicated. It's simply an exercise in seeing ourselves and the world around us more clearly. And it is obvious that we need to see ourselves more clearly through a mirror, sometimes literally. Most of the time that "mirror" can be a prompt or a question to help us look within. In its simplest form, reflection is asking yourself a question and answering it honestly. That's obviously not easy; it's much more than just getting a book of questions, a notebook, and a pen. Having a mirror is important, but it's not enough.

Let us imagine that I need to improve my disheveled appearance. Let's say, too, that you are helping me to do that. Say you bring a mirror to me. You help me unpack it and hang it up. Maybe you bring me to it and put me squarely in front of it. You may even tell me what *you* see in my face and appearance. But that's still not enough for me to see myself clearly and understand my appearance. There is one thing, at a minimum, that I must do on my own. If I want to see myself clearly, I must be curious enough to open my eyes. This is why deep change must start with us. Nobody can force us to open our eyes; that must come voluntarily.

Humility is an important idea, and over the years, and over the course of writing this volume, I have struggled to define it. But I think one way to define humility, indirectly at least, is to say that it is a willingness and desire to see ourselves clearly. By doing this we demonstrate that, though we are small and imperfect mortal men, we want to be better.

It's easy to parrot to others, even for a narcissistic man, that we are imperfect mortal men with our eyes closed. But it's quite another proposition entirely to open our eyes, look in the mirror, and admit to it after seeing it for ourselves. It is one of the hardest things for a person to do. But even that is not enough because the hardest trials come after we open our eyes. Because once we open our eyes and look in the mirror, we have to understand what we see. And not just understand what we see, but be honest about what it means. Then we must grapple with difficult questions: What does what we see compel us to do? How must we change?

When we open our eyes and see something ugly—which we will, because we are imperfect mortal men—a common reaction to have (myself included) is to blame others for it. If we can blame someone else, we are able to delude ourselves into thinking we are not responsible for what we are, and therefore it's someone else's responsibility to fix it, not ours. Then the greatest choice we will ever make presents itself: when we see something ugly in the mirror, will we remain ignorant by averting our eyes? Will we blame others? Or will we summon all our courage and make the choice to take responsibility for who we are and do something to become better, no matter how difficult it is?

I see now that this choice, the choice we make at the mirror, eyes wide open, is the first opportunity we have to choose between goodness and power. On the one hand, we can try to be better, we can accept responsibility and choose to be more good. Or, we can say no to that responsibility and try to accumulate the means and the power to avoid changing ourselves. Will we try to be better, or will we refuse? What, my sons, will you choose?

The choice made in front of the mirror comes up, in some form or another, all the time, every single day. And that, I see now, is the reason I wrote this book.

I wanted to pick apart how, over the course of a lifetime, to choose to become better, so that when I come up to the mirror, I choose differently. I want to step up to the mirror, open my eyes, and no matter what I see, I want to choose to take responsibility to be better and grow into someone more good. And I want to be able to do that, make that same choice, with persistence, again and again, and become, day by day, a better man.

I believe, with my full heart, that developing that strength of character comes by constantly exercising and expanding our curiosity, courage, and persistence. I have shared my ideas and learnings on specific ways to do that in these letters. I wanted to leave you with the most practical set of ideas and reflections I could muster because, as much as I love moral philosophy and find the great moral theories important and useful, I was at a loss for finding real, thoughtful guidance on how to actually become a good person. I didn't find the "here's how to do it in real life" sort of discussion in any of those great books. I didn't find the wisdom of a practitioner on how to build strength of character and how to become a better man, so I tried to create the book I wanted to read myself.

This volume is, in essence, my reflection on how to be a better man and a defense of why I think curiosity, courage, and persistence are the keystone virtues to being able to become a better man, intentionally, in real life. I also wanted to provide you with something practical to react to, to get you really started, so you would have a starting point for the *how* of it all rather than just the what and why.

So, my sons, let's finish on this question—the alpha and omega of where our work starts and ends: how do we open our eyes? Because, if we are able to do that, again and again, the process of deep change will start and be jumpstarted, over and over again. If we do not open our eyes, similarly, the process of deep change will never begin; it's where our work starts and ends.

I stumbled onto a book I mentioned in one of my letters that is helpful here: *The Second Mountain* by David Brooks. Let me draw from it.

In the book, Brooks talks about surrendering our lives to others. He argues that the people who do that are the ones who find true joy. Brooks, who studied joyful people, found that surrendering one's life to others happens in four distinct ways: to family; a vocation; a philosophy or faith; or a community. I honestly don't know exactly how that works. I'm not even sure if one can proactively and willfully surrender one's life to another by the snap of the fingers or by proclaiming it into existence. To answer that question is in the domain of someone wiser than me, and perhaps in the province of God rather than man. But I will say this with great conviction and devotion: I think that one way or another, even if we can't call our shot on what will draw our hearts and souls to the point of surrender, those things do find us. I will forever be faithful because family found me. Your mother found me and let me love her. Your mother found me, at the bar, at what used to be an Irish pub, and she got to know me, and she loves me. You boys found me and let me love you. I love you. I love you all so much. And you love me. In my life, what has helped me to surrender and open my eyes is *you*. You are the reason.

In the reflection that led me to write these letters to you, I realized two things: (1) that my job as a father has two primary responsibilities: to love you unconditionally, and to help you become good people; and (2) the best way to help you become good people is to become a good person myself.

The topics we have covered in these letters to you are my plan—my map of sorts—to do just that. I hope they are helpful reflections to you as well. I hope you will want to become good men, independent of my dreams for you.

207

In the twilight of these letters, the one message I want to start and end with has nothing to do with goodness or character. It has nothing to do with choices or with power. It is that I love you. I love you all more than I can reasonably write in prose. I love you much farther than to the moon and back. These letters to you, more than helping me to reflect on goodness and how to be a better man, are a reflection that helped me put into words what my love for you boys, your mother, and our family compels me to do.

The love I share with you all has been the most important change in my life. Finding my way to you, my family, is my cannonball moment, like that of St. Ignatius. This love we share is my deepest source of gratitude. The chance to love you all, your mother, and our family is the greatest honor and joy of my life. It is from this place of unconditional love that I share these reflections on goodness with you.

Thank you, my sons, for opening my eyes.

I love you,
Papa

* * *

IV

2023

20

In Closing

September 14, 2023

Dear Reader,

In some ways, this volume was never supposed to be a book. It started humbly, as something in my journal that I wrote because I was scared to be a father in a world where mine was already gone. But then, as I wrote these letters over the course of years, something magical happened. I began to discern some wisdom across the books and videos I had read and watched. Disciplines like complex systems, business, poetry, psychology, and philosophy started to connect. I have always been a dot-connector and integrator of ideas, and that's what I see this book as: a set of dots, once disparate, that became interesting and novel to me because they're now connected.

I have included a list of selected works in the final pages of this book, as well as a few blank pages with some of the most interesting questions I grappled with while writing this book. The pages are for you to fill in your own thoughts and questions.

I hope reading this conversation between my sons and me has been worthwhile to you. If you know someone who is looking for this book, exactly, I hope you share it. I would also love to hear your reactions and stories. You can get a hold of me by emailing hello@neiltambe.com.

More than anything, I hope you don't stop just at reading. I hope what I've shared here sparks something in you and that your own creative project comes out of it. Maybe it's a blog, a podcast, or a painting. I hope, too, that you find a simple question and even write your own book about it—not to be a bestseller or to become a famous author, but because you have something important to say and want to share it.

That, I think, has been the greatest lesson from my putting in the arduous work to pen this volume: we all have something important to say. We all have a story to tell. We all have a voice that's worth raising. Writing this book has been a transformative experience for me. I wish you the same blessing as you engage in your efforts to bring your own creation to the world. Good luck as you walk your own path. I will be rooting for you from Detroit.

Your friend,
Neil

* * *

Inspirations and Referenced Works

1. Art of Manliness Podcast. "#652: Chefs' Secrets for Organizing your Life." https://www.artofmanliness.c om/character/advice/mise-en-place-how-chefs-organi ze/.
2. Babbitt, Natalie. *The Search for Delicious*.
3. Brooks, David. *The Second Mountain: The Quest for a Moral Life*.
4. Brown, Brené. *Atlas of the Heart: Mapping Meaningful Connection and the Language of Human Experience*.
5. Center for Positive Organizations. "Reflected Best Self Exercise." https://reflectedbestselfexercise.com.
6. Centola, Damon. *How Behavior Spreads: The Science of Complex Contagion*.
7. Christensen, Clayton. "How will you measure your life?" YouTube.
8. Christian, Brian R., and Tom Griffiths. *Algorithms to Live By: The Computer Science of Human Decisions*.
9. Curry, Bishop Michael. "Love is the Way." YouTube.
10. De Secondat Montesquieu, Charles, and George R. Healy. *Persian Letters*.
11. Edelman. "*Edelman Trust Barometer*." https://www.edel man.com/trust/trust-barometer.
12. Farnam Street. "Avoiding Stupidity Is Easier Than

Seeking Brilliance." https://fs.blog/avoiding-stupidity/.

13. Farnam Street. "The Inner Scorecard: How Warren Buffett Mastered Life." https://fs.blog/the-inner-scorecard/.

14. Foster Wallace, David. "This is Water." Graduation Speech at Kenyon College, 2005.

15. Gates, Rolf, and Katrina Kenison. *Meditations from the Mat.*

16. Godin, Seth. Seth Godin's Blog. "Sunk costs, creativity and your Practice."https://seths.blog/2021/05/sunk-costs-creativity-and-your-practice/.

17. Gogol, Nikolai V., and David Magarshak (translator). *The Overcoat and Other Tales of Good and Evil.*

18. Gunaratana, Henepola. *Mindfulness in Plain English.*

19. His Holiness the Dalai Lama, and Archbishop Desmond Tutu. *The Book of Joy: Lasting Happiness in a Changing World.*

20. Hobbes, Thomas. *Leviathan.*

21. Juster, Norton, and Jules Feiffer (illustrator). *The Phantom Tollbooth.*

22. Kennedy, John F. *Profiles in Courage.*

23. Lahiri, Jhumpa. *Interpreter of Maladies.*

24. Lee, Harper. *To Kill a Mockingbird.*

25. MacDonald, Kathy. Professional Website. https://macdgroup.com.

26. Mayo Clinic. "Meditation: A simple fast way to reduce stress." https://www.mayoclinic.org/tests-procedures/meditation/in-depth/meditation/art-20045858.

27. National Public Radio. Talk of the Nation. "The Myth of Multitasking." https://www.npr.org/2013/05/10/182861382/the-myth-of-multitasking.

28. Orwell, George. *1984.*

29. Page, Scott. *The Difference: How the Power of Diversity Creates Better Groups, Firms, Schools, and Societies.*

30. Peet, Dr. Melissa. Generative Knowledge Institute. https://generativeknowledge.com/.

31. Plato. *The Republic.*

32. Pollan, Michael. *In Defense of Food: An Eater's Manifesto.*

33. Prabhavananda, Swāmi (translator). *Bhagavad Gita: The Song of God.*

34. Quinn, Robert E. *The Deep Change Field Guide: A Personal Course to Discovering the Leader Within.*

35. Quinn, Ryan W., and Robert E. Quinn. *Lift: Becoming a Positive Force in Any Situation.*

36. Ries, Eric. *The Lean Startup.*

37. Robinson, Marilynne. *Gilead.*

38. Rowling, J.K. *Harry Potter: The Complete Series.*

39. Scazerro, Pete. *Emotionally Healthy Spirituality: It's Impossible to be Spiritually Mature, While Remaining Emotionally Immature.*

40. Smith, Will. *Will.*

41. Steinbeck, John. *East of Eden.*

42. Tagore, Rabindranath. *Gitanjali.*

43. Tambe, Neil. Ideas From Detroit. "Radical Change Requires Radical Action." https://www.neiltambe.com/blog/2019/3/3/radical-change-requires-radical-action.

44. Tambe, Neil. Ideas From Detroit. "Temperature Check." https://www.neiltambe.com/blog/2019/1/5/temperature-check-a-marriage-tool.

45. Tolkien, J.R.R. *The Lord of the Rings.*

46. Vedantam, Shankar. "The Scarcity Trap: Why We Keep

Digging When We're Stuck in a Hole," Hidden Brain Podcast.

47. Vivekananda, Swāmi. *The Complete Works of Swami Vivekananda.*

48. Wikipedia. "Ashtanga (eight limbs of yoga)." https://en.wikipedia.org/wiki/Ashtanga_(eight_limbs_of_yoga).

49. Wikipedia. "Mark Granovetter." https://en.wikipedia.org/wiki/Mark_Granovetter#The_strength_of_weak_ties.

50. Wikipedia. "Optimism Bias." https://en.wikipedia.org/wiki/Optimism_bias.

51. Wikipedia. "Motivation." https://en.wikipedia.org/wiki/Motivation#Incentive_theories:_intrinsic_and_extrinsic_motivation.

52. Wired Magazine. "Google X Head on Moonshots: 10x Is Easier Than 10 Percent." https://www.wired.com/2013/02/moonshots-matter-heres-how-to-make-them-happen/

53. X. "Projects." https://x.company/projects/.

Gratitude

This book, like any creative work, would not have happened without the support and efforts of many others. I am grateful for everyone who was part of this team.

First, thank you to Marsha Phillips for your generous work to edit and proofread my manuscript so the signal could emerge from the noise. Thank you Keke Shen for your wonderful work to design the cover. Thank you both for the patience, kindness, and grace you gave me as a new author as I tried to figure this out.

Second, thank you to my family and friends who provided encouragement, feedback, and the confidence I needed to see this work through to the finish, especially these people: Anil Bhansali, Bob Paul, Anjali Tambe, Kathy Paul, Eric Price, Liz Davisson, Amanda Navarro, Liz Zupan, Chris Paul, Alyssa Waugh, Zak Waugh, Brendan Paul, Sara Ramaswamy, and our entire extended family. To my wife Robyn, thank you for reminding me that I had a voice worth raising, a story worth sharing, and for creating the time for me to write as we raised our three beautiful sons.

Third, thank you to Tyler Cowen, Seth Godin, Shane Parrish, Adam Grant. Dr. Becky Kennedy, Michael Schur, Dax

Shephard, Monica Padman, David Brooks, and Ezra Klein. Even though I have never met them, they have been role models from afar that have given me confidence that it's possible to share something you believe in and be yourself as you do it.

There are too many mentors to name individually who taught me to write, think, and lead. If you have ever been a coach, teacher, mentor, camp counselor, or manager of mine, thank you, truly, for pushing me to grow.

Finally, thank you to you, the reader. Time and attention are precious resources, and I appreciate you sharing some of yours with me. If you found this work valuable, I would appreciate you sharing it with others you know who might also find it valuable. You can do that by pointing them to http://www.neiltambe.com/CharacterByChoice. I've even created a version that is free to download and share.

Question Book

When I was a teenager, I made what I called "The Question Book." It was a simple spiral notebook of lined paper. I'd write a question at the top of the page, whatever I was thinking about in my heart, and write until I was done answering it. It was in those pages that I began to explore my inner world. It didn't take any special notebook, pen, or pencil. All it took was a blank page and honesty.

In this section you will find questions, one for each chapter, that I often thought about while writing this book. I share them here as thought starters for your own reflection. I intentionally left ample space on each page as an invitation for you to write and consider your own thoughts. I hope you find something valuable as you explore these questions.

What has shaped my perception of right and wrong?

Why am I here?

What do I want this community to be like?

Is being a good person worth it? Why?

How much is enough?

What do I really want to be? Good? Happy? Something else?

If I assume I was born as a curious person, what has beat it out of me?

To really slow down, what would have to be true?

What ideas do I fill my head with? Is that what I want to be learning?

What result am I trying to create?

Who do I need to forgive? What can I let go of?

What hard things have I done that have made me who I am?

I feel...

<u>Who do I truly listen to? Who am I merely pretending
to listen to?</u>

What are obscure memories I think about a lot?

What's still worth learning?

How do I define success? How does society define success?

What do I care about contributing to, even though I won't be alive when it's done?

Who am I in a conditional relationship with? Is that really right?

What do I hope for? What are my dreams?

What am I lying to myself about?

What's that thing, deep in my heart, that I need to share with the world?

Whose shoulders am I standing on? Who has poured love and time into me?

What does it look like in real life, to be good?

If I were good, what would I see when I looked in the mirror?
What do I actually see?

About the Author

Neil Tambe is a husband, father, and citizen. His writing draws from a diverse set of disciplines and experiences, including stints working in a large consultancy, public service, and corporate strategy. In addition to writing weekly posts on his long-running blog, *Ideas from Detroit*, he enjoys running, cooking, and visiting National Parks. He is an alumnus of the University of Michigan and resides in Detroit, Michigan with his wife, three sons, and their lovable lab-mix rescue dog.

Neil was first published as a news reporter and opinion columnist for *The Michigan Daily*. He has authored and co-authored research published by the *Urban Social Assembly, Deep Blue* at the University of Michigan, and *Deloitte Consulting*. This is his first book.

You can connect with me on:
- http://www.neiltambe.com
- https://www.facebook.com/ntambe
- https://www.linkedin.com/in/neiltambe

Subscribe to my newsletter:
- https://www.neiltambe.com/subscribe-2